PENGUIN HANDBOOKS

THE ART OF THE MIDDLE GAME

Paul Keres, the great Estonian chess-master, was born at Narva in 1916. He first made his mark in the international field by representing his country very successfully on first board at the Warsaw Chess Olympiad of 1935. Since then his career has been rich in victories, ranging from first prizes at Semmering-Baden in 1937 and Avro in 1938 to numerous successes in post-war years – three first places in Soviet Championships and first prize at Budapest in 1952 are the most notable. His career as a writer on chess has been equally important and he has become celebrated for his originality and capacity for thoroughness.

Alexander Kotov, one of the finest attacking players of the century, has achieved major tournament successes. He was equal first with Bronstein in the 1948 Soviet Championship, won first prize at Venice in 1950, and gained first place in the great Interzonal Tournament at Stockholm in 1952. He is also noted for his books on chess, in particular a study of Alekhine.

Harry Golombek, one of Britain's foremost international masters, is Chess Correspondent of *The Times* and the *Observer*.

D1498631

PAUL KERES AND ALEXANDER KOTOV

THE ART OF
THE MIDDLE GAME

TRANSLATED AND EDITED BY

H. GOLOMBEK

PENGUIN BOOKS

Penguin Books Ltd, Harmondsworth, Middlesex, England
Penguin Books Inc., 7110 Ambassador Road, Baltimore, Maryland 21207, U.S.A.
Penguin Books Australia Ltd, Ringwood, Victoria, Australia

—

Konsten att vinna i schack first published in Sweden 1961
The Art of the Middle Game first published in Penguin Books 1964
Reprinted 1972

—

Copyright © H. Golombek, 1964

—

Made and printed in Great Britain by
Cox & Wyman Ltd, London, Reading and Fakenham
Set in Monotype Times

CONTENTS

EDITORIAL FOREWORD

The object of this book on the game of chess is to teach the reader how to think and how to play in the middle game. It is not intended as an exhaustive and exhausting manual on the subject. That would demand some thousands of pages and in the end, by trying to deal with too much, it might defeat the purpose of the enterprise. It would become impossible to see the wood for the trees.

So what we have done is picked out certain salient aspects and, by concentrating on them, we have hoped to show the processes of thought by which the middle game is or should be played. That the subject is a difficult one appears from the comparative scarcity of books on the middle game. Books on the openings abound; nor are works on the end game wanting, but those on the middle game can be counted on the fingers of one hand.

And yet no one can deny the obvious importance of this phase of the game, or for that matter its great interest. Here, where we get the full orchestration of the game, the player has the opportunity of utilizing all his pieces to carry out his ideas. Here he has the chance of carrying out fine combinations, of initiating attacks, and of creating defensive systems; and it is undoubtedly here that hitherto he has received the least help from chess writers.

The rare authors who have in fact treated the subject have tended to run foul of two pitfalls, both of which we hope have been avoided in this book. Some, in the first, though making a genuine effort to deal with the vast practical difficulties in the middle game, bewilder themselves and their readers by an unsystematic profusion of examples. In an attempt to give as much of the whole as is humanly possible they overshoot the mark and merely make it all the more muddled than before.

The second pitfall is more insidious and it is not indeed confined to books on the middle game or indeed to books on chess in general. It lies in an endeavour to mask an essential poverty of original ideas by the use of high-flown jargon. Into such a category there comes the talk of the conversion of command of time into command of space, or vice versa. Even the great Nimzovich, who did indeed contribute much that was valuable and original to the subject, was a considerable sinner in this respect and all too often tried to conceal the barrenness of his ideas by his undoubted combinational genius.

I (if I may be allowed here to abandon the editorial 'we' for the moment) have been fortunate in the two great masters whose writings represent the bulk of the ensuing work. Neither Keres nor Kotov has been trapped by the pitfalls described above. The concentration on certain outstanding peaks of the middle game has enabled them to avoid the first, and as practising tournament players of great success and repute they have been well aware that – to use a convenient French proverb – 'one cannot pay one's way by phrases'. Hence the severely practical approach employed in this book: when theories are in fact stated they are drawn uniquely from the authors' own experiences in play. Facts have not been contorted to fit in with preconceived ideas. There are ideas in plenty but they are such as naturally arise from the positions that occur in actual play and they are presented so as to help and not in order to mystify the reader.

The introductory chapter was not part of the original work but was designed by me to pave the way to what follows and also to fill a curious gap in chess literature. For, though all are agreed on the vital necessity to form a plan in chess, none has tried to show how plans are to be formed. Yet that this is a vast gap which it is essential to fill is shown by the enormous number of games lost through failure on the part of the player either to form the right plan or to appreciate what sort of plan is appropriate to a given position. How often have we not seen a player obtain an excellent position from the opening merely to spoil it by indifferent or unplanned play in the middle game. Again it should be emphasized that no attempt has been made here to describe all the manifold types of plan that may be conceived over the chess-board. However, we hope that enough has been given to hammer in the fundamental lesson to the reader.

In choosing the topics for discussion the authors have been guided by what is most essential and occurs most often in the middle game. Since the checkmating of the King is after all the one great objective in the whole game, a whole chapter by Kotov is devoted to the study of the strategy and tactics involved in attacking the King. This too is fundamental for the make-up of a good chess-player and it is fortunate for the content of this chapter that Kotov happens to be one of the great masters of our time of the attack on the King. Hence the zest with which he deals with the subject.

The natural corollary to attack is defence and it is with this problem that Keres is concerned in the chapter that follows. However, this is no conventional treatment of an obvious subject. Keres has deliberately chosen positions that are difficult to defend in order to show how one can defend any position given the right spirit and understanding, no matter how hopeless it may seem. It is instructive to observe how such a great master of the attack (certainly one of the immortals in this respect) ever got interested in the matter of defence. When Keres started his chess career he produced such a dazzling series of brilliant attacks that some people feared his progress, though meteoric, might like the meteor end in dust and powder. But with remarkable self-knowledge he realized that defence was as important as attack, setting himself the task of becoming a complete master. Hence in his maturity he has developed into an outstanding expert in the art of defence as well as attack.

This gives us the two main themes that must dominate every middle game – attack and defence. But these two themes are themselves in a way subservient to what we may term the mechanics of the game. More and more nowadays we are realizing the truth of the statement by that eighteenth-century chess genius, Philidor, 'pawns are the soul of chess'. As Kotov demonstrates in the chapter following, the shape and configuration of the pawns in the centre have a vital bearing on the way one has to play the middle game. All good players realize this and if one wants to become a good player it is essential to learn which pawn positions favour which types of attack and defence.

It is the final chapter which I believe the reader will find most difficult to comprehend and yet most rewarding to study. It concerns the art of analysis and Keres, adopting as always a practical point of view, has taken the subject of analysis of adjourned games, so revealing how a master's mind works and how a chess-player should set about the task of analysing any given position. It is true, I suppose, that one can marvel at the colossal thoroughness with which Keres treats his analyses, without necessarily wishing to emulate him. And yet something of the spirit with which he approaches the game of chess will communicate itself to the reader if he is prepared to work through the examples with Keres as his guide.

As translator I had of necessity to study the author's texts with great care and attention, and I must confess that I myself felt the benefit of them as a chess-player. It is my fervent hope and belief that the reader will derive at least as much help from this work as I did.

H. GOLOMBEK

1

PLANNING IN THE MIDDLE GAME

H. Golombek

The distinguished authors who have written the succeeding chapters of this book have concentrated on two main objectives: the way one should think in the middle game and the manner in which the thoughts that arise during this process are translated into action.

It is of course no part of their purpose to take into account the fact that the less experienced or less advanced player of the game is faced by problems in the matter of planning that the expert and the more advanced players take for granted in the course of play. The beginner is not even aware of the vital necessity of forming a plan; or, if he does realize it, has not the slightest idea how he should start to set about it.

It is to fill this gap that I have written this chapter. The more advanced player may therefore, if he likes, by-pass this introduction to the ensuing studies of the art of the middle game and go straight on to the deeper work of Keres and Kotov. However, I must add the word of warning to those who wish to do this that I have seen even players of master strength who have sinned against the fundamental rules of planning in chess, so meeting with disaster.

In order to illustrate my theme I will draw upon my own experiences in match and tournament play, not so much because I might consider my own games to be necessarily more interesting, rather because it is easier to explain one's ideas through one's own play, so giving the reader a complete picture of the state of play.

NECESSITY OF A PLAN

A fundamental necessity both for a successful attack and a correct defence is the formation of a sound plan, and the logical adherence to this plan despite any seductive alternatives that may present themselves during the course of play. Two sure ways of spoiling a good attack or of collapsing in defence lie in adopting a piecemeal policy, or, still worse, in simply drifting. To play from move to move is obviously reprehensible but the tendency to drift is more insidious. In fact, we may be conscious that we are so doing and still continue to commit the crime. For crime it is and a sign of its importance and its ill effect on one's play lies in the undoubted fact that the great players rarely drift. This characteristic is, indeed, one way of distinguishing the great master from the ordinary player. There is no impression of drift in his moves; on the contrary, they fit into a logical pattern so as to form a deep plan that dominates the whole game.

Look at the games of the great players of the past – Alekhine, Capablanca, Lasker, Rubinstein, Steinitz, Morphy, and Anderssen – or of those of the present – Botvinnik, Keres, Tal, and Fischer – and you will realize how the formation of a correct plan forms the basis of all their winning attacks and accurate defences.

One can go even farther and point out that a really interesting game is not just a one-sided encounter in which one player's plan triumphs against a player without any; nor does it merely depend on two good players facing each other, but it does occur when you get two good plans clashing against each other, if one may be allowed to personify them. Crushing victories in under twenty moves soon begin to pall and the chief drawback in the collected games of such players as Anderssen and Morphy lies in the inferior nature of the opposition. The players they met went like lambs to the slaughter – *sans* plan *sans* everything.

In the international field nowadays most players are fully aware of the necessity of forming a plan; but they tend to err by virtue of the fickle nature of humanity. By this I mean that they will go astray through a fitful handling of the attack or of the defence. They will start on one plan, switch over to another that seems more attractive, and then, when it is too late, try to return to the original plan.

As a good example of this fits-and-starts policy consider the following game that was played in the Golden Sands Olympiad of 1962.

Queen's Pawn, King's Indian Defence

WHITE: GOLOMBEK   BLACK: G. PUIG

1.	P – Q4	Kt – KB3
2.	P – QB4	P – KKt3
3.	Kt – QB3	B – Kt2
4.	P – K4	O – O
5.	P – B3	P – B4

Already the nature of Black's plan has defined itself. He is prepared to allow White a certain pawn preponderance in the centre provided that in return he is able to concentrate on a counter-attack on the Queen's side: an excellent plan that has proved its worth in many a modern game and one that would work here too – always provided Black sticks to his plan.

6.	P – Q5	P – Q3
7.	B – Q3	P – K3
8.	KKt – K2	P × P
9.	BP × P	

Now White's plan is clear. He intends to utilize his pawn majority in the centre to make a thrust there; hence he recaptures with the BP rather than the KP so as to have in reserve the eventual advance of P – K5. A basic rule in middle-game planning is that, other things being equal, the advance in the centre will have a more powerful effect than the advance on the flank. Readers should bear in mind my proviso of other things being equal since it covers, for instance, such cases where one side or the other has made some weakening move on the King's or Queen's wing which may be more immediately and severely punished by an advance on the wing in question.

9.	....	Kt – R3
10.	O – O	Kt – QKt5

13

The first change in plan. Black, lured away by the possibility of attacking White's K Bishop, neglects to follow the logical line of counter-attack on the Queen's side. He should have played *10. ..... Kt – B2*, aiming at the advance of the QKtP, which can be carried out eventually by **P – QR3** and **R – QKt1**.

11.	B – QB4	R – K1
12.	P – QR3	Kt – R3
13.	B – KKt5	

White has not only mere development in mind with this move. If Black drives away the Bishop by P – KR3 and P – KKt4 then he will have weakened his King's side and driven the Bishop to a post from which it can aid the central pawn thrust of P – K5. There is also a more insidious notion in the move – it is designed to induce Black to change his plan yet once more.

13.	....	Q – Kt3

And Black does exactly this; he forms a fresh plan with the idea of unpinning himself and then manoeuvring the QKt – Q2 so as to hold back the advance of White's KP. That this plan utterly fails is due to the waste of time caused by Black's constant change of plan.

14.	Q – Q2	Kt – Kt1
15.	Kt – Kt3	QKt – Q2
16.	P – B4	P – KR3
17.	B – R4	Kt – Kt5
18.	QR – K1	

All part of the plan of central advance. Now White is threatening to play **P – K5** followed, if Black replies P × P, by **P – Q6**. Hence Black decides to return his Knight to KB3 so as to strengthen the King's side.

18.	....	KKt – B3
19.	K – R1	Kt – R2

Puig

H. Golombek

With this move Black deems that he has adequately guarded his K4 and prevented White's central advance. But now comes the logical follow-up of White's plan.

    20. P – K5!   P – Kt4

Desperation; but what else can Black do? If he plays *20. ...* P × P, then *21.* P – Q6, threatening among other things Kt – Q5 is quite deadly.

    21. BP × P   RP × P
    22. P – K6!

A good illustration of White's theme – the central pawn advance. The plan has won through and it only remains to gather the fruits.

22.	P – B3
23. B – Kt5	P × B
24. Kt – B5	B – B1
25. P × Kt	R × R
26. R × R	B × P
27. B × B	R – Q1
28. B – K6 ch	K – R1
29. Kt × RP	resigns.

A case of too many plans spoiling the broth.

15

HOW TO FORM A PLAN

The reader may here ask: how does one form a plan in the first place? It is all very well talking of the dangers of too many plans, but what are the grounds upon which a single plan is formed, where in fact does the inspiration lie? To answer these questions I must first point out a fallacy that seems to govern all our textbooks on chess. According to these chess is divided into three watertight compartments: the opening, the middle game, and the ending, each phase being entirely divorced from the rest of the game. Naturally, this was not the original intention of the authors of our manuals on chess. Chess was so divided for convenience's sake, in order to make it easier to treat of each phase clearly and without embarrassing the student by making complicated references to the interrelation of the one phase with the other.

But there is no doubt that the process of separation has been pushed too far. It must be emphasized that one of the qualities of the game of chess that serves to make it at once more interesting and more difficult is the interrelation of the three main phases of play: opening, middle game, and ending. In playing the opening one has always to bear in mind what effect the way one handles the early part of the game will have on the middle game, and in conducting this latter phase one must equally consider how it will affect the ending.

Most books on the openings are positively dangerous for the development of the young and aspiring player since they ignore this important fact. What often happens is that your promising young player will memorize a variation that ends with a plus-minus in White's favour, and then expect the rest of the game to play itself. All the greater his disappointment and surprise when the game refuses to do any such thing; in no time at all his plus-minus becomes first an equals, then a minus-plus, and finally a dead loss. This is not to imply that a study of the openings is useless – far from it. But it must be undertaken in the awareness that the opening is directly followed by the middle game and that the choice of an opening variation will have an immense influence on one's plan of play in later stages in the game.

This plan in fact must arise naturally and logically out of the opening. Here is the clue to the methods one must use in forming a plan and the way one must develop this plan.

I have said that what sort of influence the opening will have on the middle game depends on the nature of the opening one chooses, and in this respect the pawn skeleton is of the utmost significance. From the pawn skeleton one can deduce what pieces can or cannot be developed easily, where the attack or counter-attack can be delivered, and what sort of defensive system can be constructed.

Consider, for example, the half-open defences to the King's Pawn. The opening moves of these at once define the type of pawn skeleton for the whole game, and this in turn tells us a great deal about the kind of middle game that will result from the opening. The first few moves of the French Defence – 1. P – K4, P – K3; 2. P – Q4, P – Q4 – signify a clash in the centre where Black has already instituted a violent counterattack. His plan will be to strike at the base of White's advanced centre, which may be Q4 or QB3 according to circumstances. White on the other hand will be using his advanced centre to aid him in an attack on the King and here he will also be helped by the fact that Black's pawn skeleton shuts in his QB, thereby depriving it of any real future.

In this respect, compare the Caro-Kann Defence. Here the Q Bishop is not shut in for Black, an advantage over the French Defence. There is, too, just as acute a clash in the centre as in the other defence, but the passive position of the pawn on QB3, where it deprives the Q Knight of its natural developing square, tends to produce a more defensive and passive type of game for Black than the French.

It is no exaggeration to say that Black's middle-game plan (his main one at any rate) is clear from the very first move in the Sicilian Defence: 1. P – K4, P – QB4. The bold counter-attack on White's Q4 shows that Black is, or should be, animated by a spirit of aggression from the very start. When, as nearly always occurs, White plays an eventual P – Q4 in order to gain control of this vital central square, Black will exchange off pawns and try for pressure along the QB file.

Switching over to the Queen-side openings we can readily see how the best defences there prescribe clear-cut and well-thought-out plans of play for the middle game. The most popular of late has been the King's Indian Defence: *1*. P – Q4, Kt – KB3; *2*. P – QB4; P – KKt3; *3*. Kt – QB3, B – Kt2. Here Black's heart and soul must be concentrated in the effort to obtain pressure on the black squares and so enhance the value and scope of his K Bishop. His pawn will advance to Q3, thereby helping to solve the problem of the development of his other Bishop; and then will come another pawn thrust, either K4 or QB4, so as to increase the pressure already mentioned.

In quite a number of other defences to the Queen's Pawn, Black's plan (which is carried on into the middle game) lies in endeavouring to gain control of White's K4. Three main defences are of this type: the Nimzovich Defence, *1*. P – Q4, Kt – KB3; *2*. P – QB4, P – K3; *3*. Kt – QB3, B – Kt5; the Queen's Indian Defence, *1*. P – Q4, Kt – KB3; *2*. P – QB4, P – K3; *3*. Kt – KB3, P – QKt3, followed by the placing of the QB along the long diagonal; and finally the Dutch Defence, *1*. P – Q4, P – KB4. This last defence has as its main plan the utilization of control of White's K4 to launch out on a dangerous attack against White's King. Here, however, the pawn skeleton reveals to us an inherent weakness; the fact that the KBP is placed immediately on a white square means that Black will experience considerable difficulty in developing his Q Bishop, and this in turn will make it difficult for him to develop his whole Queen's side.

So White's middle-game plan against the Dutch Defence positions consists largely in taking advantage of Black's bad QB and in frustrating his opponent's development of his Queen's side. As an illustration of the type of plan in this respect I give a game I played in a county match in 1962.

Queen's Pawn, Dutch Defence

WHITE: GOLOMBEK   BLACK: F. PARR
    1. P – Q4   P – KB4
    2. P – KKt3

Already the outline of White's plan is visible; he places his KB on the long diagonal in order to make it as hard as possible for Black to develop his Q Bishop.

2.	....	Kt – KB3
3.	B – Kt2	P – K3
4.	Kt – KB3	B – K2
5.	O – O	O – O
6.	P – B4	Q – K1
7.	Kt – B3	P – Q3
8.	P – Kt3	Q – R4

A case where the plan that Black has formed is insufficient. He attempts to attack on the King's side in an endeavour to utilize the aggressive nature of his pawn position there. But he is trying to do this without the aid of the Queen-side pieces and as a result White has little difficulty in repelling the attack. Better is 8. .... P – QR4, in order to play Kt – QR3 and eventually Kt – QKt5.

9.	P – K3	P – KKt4
10.	B – QR3	P – R4
11.	Kt – K5	Q – K1

An ignominious retreat; but after 11. .... Q × Q; 12. KR × Q, QKt – Q2; 13. Kt – Q3, Black would still experience great difficulty in developing his Queen-side pieces, while White would have a ready-made attack on that wing by Kt – QKt5 and P – B5.

12.	Kt – Q3	QKt – Q2
13.	P – B4	Kt – Kt5
14.	Q – K2	B – B3
15.	Kt – Kt5	Q – Q1
16.	P – R3	Kt – R3
17.	P × P	

It is necessary for White to divert the Black Bishop from its attack on Q4 in order to be able to advance in the centre with P – K4. This move would be bad if carried out at once on account of 17. .... P – B3.

| 17. .... | B × KtP |
| 18. P – K4 | |

All part of White's plan for exploiting Black's inability to develop his Queen-side pieces: the Rook that is developed, Black's K Rook, is to be exchanged, while White brings his own QR to bear on the King's side.

18.	P × P
19. R × R ch	Q × R
20. Q × P	Kt – B3
21. Q – K2	Kt – B4

White was threatening to win the KB by P – R4 and this move gives it a square for retreat; but it also results in loss in material and 21. .... Kt – K1 was essential, though even then the further progress of White's plan by 22. R – KB1, would leave Black miserably placed.

F. Parr

H. Golombek

| 22. P – KKt4 | Kt – R5 |

If 22. .... B – K6 ch; 23. K – R2, B × P; 24. R – KB1, P – B3; 25. Kt × B, Kt × Kt; 26. Q – KB2, winning a piece.

23. Kt × BP	R – Kt1
24. Kt × P	Q – K2
25. R – K1	B × Kt

Note that Black manages to develop this Bishop only when it is too late and the issue of the game is already decided. Also hopeless is *25.* .... Kt × B; *26.* K × Kt, B – R3; *27.* P – Kt5, B × P; *28.* Kt × B, Q – Kt2; *29.* K – R2, when White again wins a piece.

26. Q × B ch	Q × Q
27. R × Q	R – K1
28. R × R ch	Kt × R
29. B × KtP	B – K6 ch
30. K – B1	resigns

He loses yet another pawn after *30.* .... B × P; *31.* B – B6.

Hardly any opening leaves such a clear-cut impression on the subsequent course of the game or dictates so much what policy one should adopt in the middle game as the Sicilian Defence. This applies both to the variation where Black fianchettoes his King-side Bishop or to the lines where he plays it to K2. In both cases he must pay particular attention to the black squares in the centre where both his strength and his weakness lie.

The point of this seeming paradox appears most clearly in the variation *1.* P – K4, P – QB4; *2.* Kt – KB3, P – K3. Black's plan springs very readily from the nature of the pawn skeleton. He has weakened himself to a certain extent on both Q3 and K4 by the single-square advance of the KP and must make sure that White does not obtain a firm hold on either or on both of these squares. Always bearing this in mind, he will group his pieces so that they aid him in countering White's pressure on these points and, as a counter-stroke, he will try to break through on the QB file where he has a ready-made battering ram in the shape of the pawn on QB4.

White, too, has problems in the centre. If he advances his KBP, as he must do if he wishes to gain a King-side attack, then his KP is liable to become weak, or, if not weak, then open to attack. If he plays the pawn to K5, then he must be sure that in so doing he does not weaken himself along the diagonal stretching from his KR1 to QR8. Quite often the Black QB will establish itself on this diagonal: at one fell swoop this piece, normally merely a hindrance, is converted to a grave menace.

Another usual and most vigorous plan for White in his furtherance of a King-side attack in this variation lies in the advance of his flank pawns on the King's side, more particularly the KKtP. Here, too, aggression must be nicely judged and timed. If White is not extremely careful he may suddenly find he has opened up the King's side to his opponent's advantage.

The two rival plans, White aiming at a King-side attack and Black striving for a breakthrough on the QB file, are well illustrated by the following game which I played in the Northern Open Tournament at Whitby, 1963.

Sicilian Defence

WHITE: W. R. MORRY	BLACK: H. GOLOMBEK
1. P – K4	P – QB4
2. Kt – KB3	P – K3
3. P – Q4	P × P
4. Kt × P	Kt – KB3
5. Kt – QB3	P – Q3
6. P – KKt3	

A scheme of play designed to put pressure on the white squares in the centre. Its drawback, as opposed to, say, B – K2, is that it leaves Black with good possibilities of establishing a piece on his QB5.

6.	P – QR3
7. B – Kt2	Q – B2
8. O – O	B – K2
9. P – KR3	O – O
10. B – K3	B – Q2
11. Q – Q2	Kt – B3
12. P – B4	QR – B1

Already the two plans are clear; White is advancing his King-side pawns in the hope of gaining an attack there, while Black is busy preparing his counter-assault on the QB file.

13. Q – B2	

After this, one of the disadvantages of advancing the KBP which has been already mentioned, the weakening of the KP, becomes apparent. Better, therefore, would be Kt – Kt3 here, avoiding the manoeuvre Black succeeds in putting into operation on his fourteenth and fifteenth moves.

13.	P – QKt4

Black would like to play *13.* .... Kt – QR4 followed by Kt – B5, but he cannot do so at once on account of *14.* Kt × P, P × Kt; *15.* B – Kt6.

14. P – R3	Kt × Kt
15. B × Kt	B – B3
16. QR – Q1	

The obvious, but not the best move; here he should play *16.* QR – K1, since his Rooks are best placed on KB1 and K1 both for defence and attack.

16.	Q – Kt2
17. KR – K1	P – QR4
18. P – K5	

Forced, since Black was threatening P – Kt5.

18.	P × P
19. P × P	

After *19.* B × P, B × B,; *20.* Q × B, Q × Q ch; *21.* K × Q, P – Kt5; Black's plan of breaking through on the QB file would be absolutely successful.

19.	Kt – Q2
20. Kt – K4	P – B4
21. P × P e.p.	Kt × P
22. Q – K2	

The Queen must be moved away from the masked attack by the Black Rook; for if *22.* Kt – B5, B × Kt; *23.* B × B, Kt – K5; and Black wins.

22.	Kt × Kt
23. B × Kt	B × B
24. Q × B	Q × Q
25. R × Q	R × P

So Black's plan has triumphed; he has broken through on the QB file and established a Rook on the seventh rank. White can indeed restore material equality for the moment, but he is still lost as Black has too many threats on his position.

26. R × P	B – Kt4
27. R – K5	

Only superficially good, but he is without a satisfactory move. If 27. B – B3, R – KB6, and Black wins.

H. Golombek

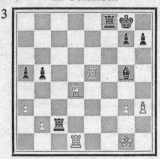

W. R. Morry

27.	B – B3
28. R – Q5	

And not 28. R × P, on account of 28. .... R – Q1, when Black wins a piece.

28.	B × B ch
29. R(Q5) × B	R × P

The first fruits of Black's occupation of the seventh rank; but there are more to come.

30. R – Q7	R – B6
31. R – Q8 ch	K – B2
32. R(Q8) – Q7 ch	K – Kt3
33. R(Q7) – Q6 ch	R – B3
34. R(Q6) – Q4	P – R4

Preventing White from playing R – Kt4 ch and providing his King with an escape square on KR2 if necessary. White's position is now hopeless and the remaining moves need no comment: *35.* P – Kt4, P – KR5; *36.* P – Kt5, R – B6; *37.* R × P, R – Kt6 ch; *38.* K – R1, R × QRP; *39.* R – R8, K × P; *40.* R – Kt1 ch, K – B3; *41.* R – B1 ch, K – K4; *42.* R – K1 ch, K – Q3; *43.* R – KKt1, P – R5; *44.* R – R5, R – K6; White resigns.

Another common and indeed principal way in which the plan for the middle game springs from the opening lies in the idea of centralization. For all openings are recognized as sound by chess theory in so far as they constitute the struggle for some very important central square and, logically enough, this struggle is carried on to the middle game, only to be concluded when the issue of the game itself is decided.

The plan, then, of concentration on the possession of an important central square is both a plan for an opening and a plan for a middle game. Provided a player is fully aware of his objective at an early stage in the game then his middle-game policy is plain. It will be the occupation and control of a central square and this may be Q4 or K4, Q5 or K5, depending on either how ambitious a player he is or else whether he is a King's-pawn or a Queen's-pawn player. Thus, both the Ruy López and the King's Gambit are assaults by White on Black's K4, in the first case more indirectly by Kt – KB3 and B – QKt5, and in the second by the violent attack P – KB4. Similarly the Queen's Gambit consists primarily of an attack on Black's Q4 by P – QB4, an attack which becomes even more insistent in the Catalan System when the King's Bishop is placed on KKt2 in order to enhance the pressure on the QP. Such an attack is even more immediate in the English Opening when, by playing *1.* P – QB4, White announces his intention of aiming at control of his Q5 square above everything. How valid this is for the middle game too can be seen very clearly in most games that start with the English Opening. In their case play consists supremely of an attack on the white squares in the centre.

Just as marked (and just as significant for middle-game planning) is the struggle for vital central squares in the standard defences. So, for example, in the French Defence, White tries to gain possession of the K5 square, while Black usually counterattacks on White's supporting square on Q4. A similar conflict may arise out of the Caro-Kann, while in the Sicilian Defence White aims first at control of his Q4 square and then, more ambitiously, of his Q5. Note that here in point of time the Q4 square control is essentially an opening plan and the Q5 square control a middle-game plan.

Turning to the Queen's side, we have already observed that the Nimzovich Defence results in a concentrated effort on both sides to obtain complete possession of White's K4, and it is noticeable that whichever side gains control of this square almost invariably succeeds in winning the game as well.

The strategic struggle for central squares is best demonstrated in those middle-game positions that arise out of every type of opening (or perhaps defence is a better word) where Black plays a King's fianchetto, i.e. where he plays B – KKt2. In positions that arise out of the King's Indian Defence, the Grünfeld Defence, and the Robatsch Defence, Black is striving with might and main to weaken White on White's Q4, that is, on the central black square. White, on the other hand, endeavours to strengthen his own Q4 as much as possible and, again with the greater ambition in mind, tries to gain command of his Q5. Once this last objective has been achieved, White has won the strategic battle and is well on the way to victory.

Thus the plan in the following game, which was played in a county match in 1963, consists for Black in attacking White's Q4, for White in gaining control of Q5; once White attains his objective Black's game falls to pieces.

Queen's Pawn, Grünfeld Defence

WHITE: H. GOLOMBEK   BLACK: J. K. FOOTNER

1. P – Q4	Kt – KB3
2. P – QB4	P – KKt3
3. Kt – QB3	P – Q4
4. P – K3	B – Kt2
5. P × P	Kt × P
6. B – QB4	

White's first assault on the Q5 square; Black has already made his intentions clear by placing his KB on Kt2 and by opening up the Q file, all so as to put pressure on White's Q4.

6.	Kt – Kt3
7. B – Kt3	O – O
8. Kt – B3	Kt – R3

Why here rather than on B3? Because Black wishes to pursue his strategic line of attack on White's Q4 by P – QB4.

9. O – O	P – QB4
10. P – QR4	

A strong move that is indirectly concerned with the control of Q5 and is a clear improvement on *10.* P – KR3, P × P; *11.* P × P, Kt – B2; *12.* R – K1, B – K3; when Black has full control of his Q4 square (Simonson–Evans, New York, 1951). Now, however, White always has in reserve the thrust P – R5 which undermines Black's central control.

10.	B – Kt5
11. P – KR3	P × P
12. P × P	

And not *12.* P × B, P × Kt; when Black has the advantage owing to the increased range of his King's Bishop.

12.	B × Kt

He decides to accept the pawn sacrifice; but White's attack grows too strong after this as does his pressure on the Q5 square, and Black would have been better advised to play the discreet *12.* .... B – B4.

13. Q × B   Q × P

Black would have a very bad game after 13. .... B × P;
14. R – Q1, when White would be threatening both B – K3 and
Kt – Kt5 and Black could not well play 14. .... P – K4 on
account of 15. B – R6.

14. P – R5   Q – QKt5
15. B – R2

And not 15. P × Kt, Q × B; 16. Q × P, Kt – B4; 17.
Q × KP, P × P; when Black has the advantage. The reader will
note how important it is to stick to the plan of controlling Q5.

15. ....   Kt – B5
16. Kt – Q5

Now Q5 is firmly in White's hands; the strategic purpose has
been fulfilled and it only remains to work out the tactical
exploitation.

16. ....   Kt – K4
17. Q – KKt3   Q × RP

Or 17. .... Q – Q3; 18. B – KB4, and the permanent pin,
with the threat of R – K1, is decisive. White can now win a
pawn back by Kt × P ch, but he has a much stronger move that
utilizes to the full his positional advantage of two Bishops.

J. K. Footner

H. Golombek

18. B – Kt5	P – K3
19. Kt – B6 ch	B × Kt

After *19.* .... K – R1; White has a winning attack by *20.* Q – R4, P – R4; *21.* B × P, Q – Kt3; *22.* B – Kt4, threatening B × RP. If then *22.* .... Kt × B; *23.* P × Kt, Q – Kt5; *24.* P – B4, Q – B4 ch; *25.* K – R1, B × Kt; *26.* B × B ch, K – Kt1; *27.* P – B5 (or even B – K7), and White wins.

20. B × B	Kt – Q2
21. B – B3	Q – R4
22. QR – Q1	Kt(R3) – B4
23. R – Q4	P – R4

Fending off White's threat of winning a piece by P – Kt4; but there is an even more deadly threat that he cannot parry.

24. R – KR4	resigns

For if *24.* .... Q – B4; *25.* B – Kt1, Q – Q4; *26.* R × P, K × R; *27.* Q – R4 ch, and mates as *27.* .... Q – R4 is not a defence owing to the pin on the KtP.

2

STRATEGY AND TACTICS OF ATTACK ON THE KING

A. Kotov

The player who has the advantage must willy-nilly go over to the attack. This principle, which was formulated by the great Steinitz, contains a number of important truths. In the first place only the player who has the advantage *can* attack. Where a positional advantage is wanting, an attack does not come into consideration at all – it is doomed to failure beforehand. In such cases one is forced to manoeuvre in the expectation that the moment may come when one has acquired so marked an advantage that one can go over to the attack. Steinitz wanted to put this a stage further: when you have an advantage you *must of necessity attack. Of necessity*. Delays are disadvantageous and even at times dangerous. When the attack comes too late the opponent can succeed in making a regrouping of his pieces to meet the attacking forces, and this means that the enemy's advantage will continually become smaller until in the end it finally disappears.

Steinitz's principle, therefore, must be understood as an imperative in accordance with which the player must regulate his play. It is not a question of what he wishes or desires – to attack or content himself with waiting manoeuvres – but of what he is compelled to do if he wants to construct from his position an intrinsic basis of chess strategy.

In fact, once a player has ascertained that he has an advantage, he must determine where the attack shall be launched. A means of determining this problem is naturally to be found in the peculiarities of the position and in its most important positional factors. One must strike where the opponent is weakest, where he has his vulnerable points. Naturally, the placing of the attacking pieces also plays a decisive role. When all one's pieces stand on the King's wing it is difficult to rush them over quickly to the Queen's side.

Very often the attack is directed against the opponent's King. Attack on the King is not merely fascinating in itself, but it is also highly profitable. The King is the most important piece and the game is at an end once the King is checkmated. Therefore the attack on the King is the most effective and decisive way of gaining one's aim. Each beginner learns as his very first steps in the game how to attack the opponent's King, and tries to master the art of attacking methods.

The attack on the King has one outstanding feature. Whereas in the offensive on the Queen's side one must husband and save one's resources, when it comes to an attack on the King one should spare nothing. The objective in a Queen's-wing attack is to win material advantages; the aim in an attack on the King is to deliver checkmate. One can sacrifice all the pieces and still give checkmate with one solitary pawn. It is just this concrete aim in a King-side attack that furnishes its especial attraction and provides opportunities for the most unexpected sacrifices and for beautiful combinations. As is generally known, the most beautiful games are in fact differentiated from other games by a breathtaking King-side attack. Attacks on the King can be separated into the following types:

1. The players have castled on opposite sides = attack on opposite castled positions;
2. The players have castled on the same side = attack on the same castled positions;
3. Attack against the uncastled King.

This division is by no means a purely formal one, but all three cases demand their particular attacking methods. We will examine the strategy and tactics of these three categories in turn and supplement the general theoretical reasoning by concrete examples taken from the storehouse of chess-master practice.

ATTACK ON OPPOSITE CASTLED POSITIONS

Even as a boy, when I was at the beginning of my career as a chess-player, I found I had to acquire for myself as thorough a mastery as possible of the practice and theory of play in positions of opposite castling. When I stayed behind at school with my school friends after lessons, and managed to play up to a hundred games in a single afternoon, the strategy was simple enough: I castled on the opposite side in the middle of violent (and mutual) King attacks. Whoever got his attack in first, won. The result was that I acquired an unfailing mastery of those positions where castling takes place on opposite sides, and from that time on I knew how to find my way about them. Later, I formulated the basic rules for strategy and tactics in such positions and I would like to elucidate for the reader the most important of these rules.

As we shall see later, attack on positions with castling on the same side proceeds with the help of play with the pieces. Quite otherwise is the procedure when the Kings find themselves at opposite corners of the board. There the attacker not only can but must carry out the attack with pawns. When our King, for example, is placed on the King's wing we can without much trouble advance the pawns on the Queen's wing without exposing our own King by this. Thus an important element of a strong attack is brought into operation. In the first place, pawns are the cheapest material in the game of chess, and this makes it advantageous to press the attack on the opponent's position with their help; in the second place, a pawn sacrifice can clear the way for the major pieces, above all for the Rooks. It takes from five to seven moves before one's own pawns come into contact with the adversary's. While this is occurring, the same process is taking place on the opposite wing, where the opponent will be storming forward with his pawns against our King. Now comes the vital question: who will be the quickest? The player who completes this assault process first in consequence acquires the initiative. He forces his opponent to interrupt the attack on the other side of the board, and obliges him instead to post his pieces in passive defence. Thus speed plays a most significant role in the pawn storm. This is why an offensive with pawns must be calculated with the same careful deliberation that one uses in assessing a combination.

When you want to set a pawn offensive in motion, or before

that while you are still meditating castling on the opposite side
to that of your opponent, you must observe the following precepts:

1. Success in a pawn attack goes to whoever is the first
   to be able to seize the initiative, or, alternatively, to
   whoever is first to force the opponent to go on the
   defensive;
2. In planning a pawn storm one must think out and determine precisely whether the opponent may not anticipate
   one and force one to suffer a lasting defensive;
3. While advancing pawns on the one wing one must
   keep one's eyes open for any opportunity of creating
   difficulties for the opponent in his pawn storm on the
   other side of the board. When it becomes necessary one
   can with advantage make one or more defensive moves;
4. One must bear in mind that in cases of opposite-side
   castling one has burnt one's boats and that as a consequence play in such positions demands concrete
   positional judgement and an exact calculation.

How then can one know when one should anticipate the
opponent with one's own attack? What factors in the contest
are decisive for a successful pawn storm? Here we will attempt
to elucidate these important questions concerning the strategy
in positions with opposite-side castling.

1. Position of the attacking pawns

We are at once confronted by some very important questions:
When should the first moves of the offensive be made? Should
the pawns be doubled or isolated? Can they move from their
original place without great loss? Does their advance weaken
the position of the pieces?

One must arrive at an entirely objective appraisal of these
factors. Sometimes scattered, isolated pawns can accomplish
their offensive tasks with much greater success than so-called
'good' pawns. Here is an example. The position in Diagram 5
is taken from a game between Konstantinopolsky and Frank,
played at Leningrad, 1935. At the first glance it seems as though

Black should arrive at a pawn attack first on the grounds of the advanced White pawns on QB4 and QKt3 and also because he has 'good' pawns. But instead the isolated and scattered White pawns on the King's wing take over the task of destroying the enemy position.

Frank

Konstantinopolsky

1.	P – R5
2. P – B4	P × P
3. P × P	P – QKt4
4. P × P	B – K3
5. P – R5	

It is of considerable importance for White's attack that the Black KKt pawn has been advanced, so providing great assistance to the White pawns in their aim to exchange on KKt6 and open up lines on the King's wing.

5.	B × P
6. QR – Kt1	R – R2
7. P – B5!	

Black has not obtained anything concrete. The pawn on QKt5 is still alive and kicking; it stands adequately guarded and meanwhile Black's King's position collapses completely.

| 7. . . . . | Q – R1 |
| 8. B – Q3 | P – B4 |

Now White gets the opportunity of spreading confusion in the enemy camp. But other continuations too are of little help to Black.

9.	P – Kt6!	R – Kt2
10.	Kt – K4	Kt × Kt
11.	B × Kt	Q – R5
12.	B × R	

White has already won a Rook and Black's attack has still hardly got into motion. It is interesting to note that White defers for so long the final capture on KKt6 and that the mere threat of exchanging forces. Black to lose a piece. A beautiful illustration of the precept 'the threat is stronger than the execution'.

12.	. . . .	Q – B5 ch
13.	K – Kt1	R – Kt1
14.	RP × P	RP × P
15.	B × B	and White soon won.

The following example is taken from the seventeenth game in the first World Championship match between Alekhine and Bogolyubov in 1929.

Bogolyubov

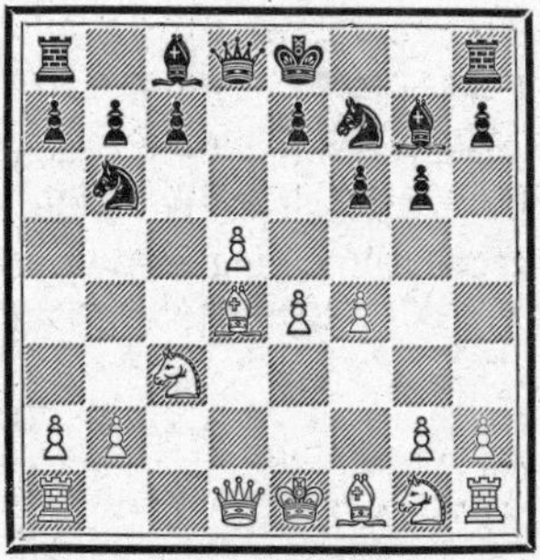

Alekhine

Alekhine began an assault with his flank pawn on the Queen's side. The advance had as its aim the constriction of the enemy pieces, but behind this there also lay a deeper objective.

With his usual intuitive imagination Alekhine perceived that Black would shortly be compelled to castle on the Queen's side and that a far advanced White pawn on QR6 would then be of great help to the White pieces in an attack on the Black King. When such a move has a double aim, this provides the most convincing proof of its correctness; in addition, a move of this sort contributes towards an immediate solution of the strategic problem. So now the pawn march P – QR4 – 5 – 6 thoroughly constricts Black's pieces and prepares for an attack on the King in the event of Black's Queen-side castling.

1.	P – QR4	P – K4
2.	P × P e.p.	B × P
3.	P – R5	Kt – Q2
4.	P – R6	P – Kt3

If Black captures on R3 then his pawns become weak and White obtains an important open Rook file.

5.	B – Kt5	Q – K2
6.	KKt – K2	P – QB4
7.	B – B2	O – O – O

This bold move was absolutely necessary. Had Black castled King-side then after 8. Kt – Q5, B × Kt; (8. . . . . Q – Q3; 9. Kt (K2) – B3), 9. Q × B, KR – Q1; 10. O – O – O, Kt – B1; 11. Q – Kt7, his position would have become particularly weak.

Now Alekhine sets in motion the decisive storming of the Black King's position, in which the pawn that has advanced so rapidly to QR6 succeeds in playing an important role. It helps in making White's attack so strong that it is impossible to beat it back.

8.	Q – R4	P – B4
9.	P – K5	P – Kt4
10.	B – B4 !	

Now he threatens a deadly check on QB6. But Bogolyubov, who does not want to die without putting up a fight, finds an intriguing piece sacrifice.

10.	Kt (Q2) × P!
11. B × B ch	Q × B
12. P × Kt	Kt × P
13. O – O	Q – B5

Black hopes to exchange Queens and thus win a third pawn for his piece. Alekhine will have nothing to do with so prosaic a continuation – he is intent on catching the Black King.

> *14.* P – QKt4 !

If now *14.* .... P × P; then there follows *15.* Kt – Kt5! Q × Kt(K7); *16.* KR – K1, Q – Q7; *17.* Kt × P ch, K – Kt1; *18.* Kt – B6 ch, and White wins.

14.	Q × KtP
15. Q – B2 !	

Alekhine has opened up the QKt file and produced the dangerous threats of *16.* R – R4, and *16.* Q × P ch. These threats can be warded off in only one way by Black.

15.	Kt – Q6
16. KR – Kt1	Q – QB5
17. R – R4	Q – K3

Other moves also lead to a loss. After *17.* .... Q – B2 White decides the issue by *18.* B – Q4! P × B; *19.* Kt – Q5 dis ch, Kt – B4; *20.* Kt × P ch, P × Kt; *21.* R × P, followed by *22.* P – R7.

18. Kt – Kt5	K – Kt1

A little better would have been 18. Kt × B; but even then *19.* K × Kt, K – Kt1; *20.* Kt – Kt3, KR – B1; *21.* R – R3, would have maintained White's strong attack.

19. Kt(K2) – Q4	Q – K5
20. Kt(Kt5) – B3	Q – K1
21. Q × Kt	P × Kt
22. B × P	Q – K3
23. Q – B3	Q – B2
24. B × P	resigns.

After *24.* .... P × B; *25.* R × P ch, K – B1; *26.* Q – B6 ch, Q – B2; *27.* R – Kt8 ch, K × R; *28.* P – R7 ch, White mates in two moves.

Yet another example that has already become classical. Diagram 7 contains a position from the game Riumin–Euwe in the Leningrad Tournament of 1934.

Euwe

Riumin

White's pieces are beautifully developed whereas the Black pieces on the Queen's wing are frozen in immobility. These circumstances afford White a decisive advantage in his pawn attack on the King's side.

1. P – KR4	Q – R3
2. P – KKt4!	

Observe how cleverly Riumin prepares the pawn storm. Without having as yet castled he makes some moves with his pawns on the wing where he intends to attack. In consequence his infantry is well prepared for the decisive storming of Black's defensive bulwarks.

2.	Kt – B4
3. Q – Q2	P – QKt3

Euwe is still unable to conjecture on what side his opponent intends to castle. The consequence is that the Black pawns on the Queen's wing still stand fixed in their starting-positions, whereas the White pawns already appear at the gate of the enemy citadel.

4. O – O – O   B – Kt2
5. P – Kt5   Q – K3

It is interesting to note how White wins a couple of tempi for the assault through attacking the unfortunately placed Black Queen.

6. Q – Q4   Q – B2
7. P – R5   Kt – K3
8. Q – Q3   Kt – B4
9. Q – Q2   P – B6

A last attempt to complicate the struggle. After *10.* B × BP, B – B5; *11.* P – K3, B × KP; Black does not stand so bad. But Riumin's effective retort decides the game.

Euwe

Riumin

10. P – Kt6 !!

In his commentaries on this game Euwe writes: 'If Black now captures on Kt3 then he is lost after *25.* P × P, Q × P; *26.* B × P, with the threat of *28.* QR – Kt1.'

10.	Q – B5
11. Kt × Q	B × Kt
12. P – K3	P × B
13. R – R4 !	B – Kt4
14. P × P ch	K × P
15. Q – B2 ch	K – Kt1
16. R – Kt4	

White has great material superiority and an attack into the bargain. Black cannot make any further resistance.

16. . . .	Kt – K3
17. P – B4	B – B6
18. R × KtP	resigns.

When we now examine the examples quoted it becomes apparent that White has achieved great success with his pawn attack thanks either to a consistently better preparation for assault or to a superior pawn position. The player who wants to set into action a pawn attack in positions of opposite castling must pay strict attention to his own pawn position and to the adequate preparation of his pawns for the ensuing struggle. A correct appreciation of this problem contributes largely to success in the struggle.

2. *Position of the opponent's pawns*

This problem is so self-apparent that we do not need to illustrate it with examples. It is to our advantage when the defending pawns allow us the opportunity of a speedy opening up of lines. It is for this reason, for instance, that a Black pawn on QR3 is more to our advantage than one on QR2 when we attack on the Queen's wing. If the pawn stands on QR3 we can easily open up a line of attack by pushing up a pawn to our QKt5 whereas when the enemy pawn is on QR2 we must advance our own to Kt6.

3. *Opponent's pieces in the way of the pawn attack*

When the opponent's pieces stand in the way of our advancing pawns, it is to our advantage. By an attack with the pawns on these pieces the attacker forces them to retreat and he gains tempi into the bargain for his onslaught. One should always reckon with this possibility as a neat and convenient device for accelerating the rush of the pawn storm.

We shall quote two examples on this theme. First a position from a game between Alekhine and Marshall (Baden-Baden, 1925).

Marshall

Alekhine

Alekhine plans to castle Queen-side. After having accurately weighed up all the possibilities of a pawn attack he discovers that the enemy pieces which stand in the way of the attacking White pawns go towards helping them in their offensive thrust.

| 1. Q – Q2 | B – Q2 |
| 2. Q – K3! | |

A move with many objectives. In the first place it prevents Black from castling Queen-side, and in the second it prepares for castling on that side by White himself. In addition the posting of the Queen on K3 facilitates a rapid pawn storm for White on the King's wing. It is interesting to observe how carefully Alekhine disguises his intentions. He is in a position to castle Queen-side but refrains from revealing the secret until he has made everything ready for forcing through his attack against the Black King with the maximum power.

2. . . . .   B – B3

Here Black misses his last opportunity of castling Queen-side by failing to play 2. . . . . Q – QR4. Now he must castle on the other side and there his King manages to attain temporary security.

3. O – O – O   O – O
4. P – B4

The first win of a tempo. White's attack rolls forward with great speed.

4. . . . .   Q – K3
5. P – K5   KR – K1
6. KR – K1   QR – Q1
7. P – B5

Yet another win of a tempo. Alekhine has worked out his attack with the utmost accuracy.

7. . . . .   Q – K2
8. Q – Kt5   Kt – Q4
9. P – B6   Q – B1
10. B – B4!

The White pawns have already come into contact with the Black pawns that defend the King, whereas Black has not even begun his attack on the other side of the board. One circumstance alone is decisive for the success of White's attack, namely, that he is in full possession of the initiative. Now his problem is to complete with his pieces what he has begun with his pawns.

10. . . . .   Kt × Kt
11. R × R   R × R
12. P × P!   Kt × P ch

Or 12. . . . . Q – K1; 13. B × P ch, K × B; 14. R – B1 ch, K – K3; 15. R – B6 ch, K – Q4; 16. R – B8, with an easy win for White.

Marshall

10

Alekhine

13. K – Kt1!

Attack *à la Alekhine*! After 13. B × Kt Black would have a saving check on QB4.

    13. ....   Q – K1
    14. P – K6!

Yet another White pawn joins in the fight.

    14. ....   B – K5 ch
    15. K – R1   P – KB4

Or 15. .... P × P; 16. B × P ch, Q × B; 17. Q × R ch, K × P; 18. Q – Q4 ch, followed by 19. R × B.

    16. P – K7 dis ch   R – Q4
    17. Q – B6   Q – B2
    18. P – K8 = Q ch and mates in two moves.

The following diagram is taken from the game Kan–Stepanov (U.S.S.R. Championship, 1931).

Stepanov

11

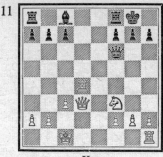

Kan

White would seem to have the more active position, but such an appreciation of the case fails to take into account one important consideration. The players have castled on opposite sides. Who will be first to achieve a pawn attack? Who will first seize the initiative? The only answer is Black. It is he who has the possibility of advancing his pawns and attacking the White pieces with gain of tempo. This circumstance is decisive in enabling Black to succeed in his attack.

1.	B – K3
2. P – QKt3	

This merely favours Black's plans. By *2.* P – QR3 he could have put up a longer resistance.

2.	P – B4

Winning a tempo for the attack.

3. R – Q6	P – QR4
4. R – Q1	P – R5
5. K – Kt2	P – QKt4

The first indication that Black's attack is succeeding – all his pawns are on the move, whereas White's pawns on the King's wing have not as yet moved forward an inch.

6. Q – K3	P – Kt5
7. Kt – K5	P × P ch
8. K × P	P × P
9. P × P	P – B5!

Black forces through his attack with great energy. He literally hacks to pieces all the defensive walls of the enemy. In view of which it is not so surprising that Black's pieces should so speedily murder the White King.

10. Q – Q4	P × P
11. Kt – B6	Q – Kt4
12. P – Kt3	KR – B1
13. P – B4	Q – R4 ch
14. K – Q3	R × Kt!

The simplest way to victory.

15. R × R	Q – Kt4 ch
16. R – B4	B × R ch
17. Q × B	R – Q1 ch
18. K – K3	Q – K1 ch
19. resigns.	

4. Pieces in the way of the opponent's advancing pawns

When our own pieces hinder the freedom of movement of our pawns, this naturally suggests that we lose time by advancing them. Therefore we must set about preparing the pawn storm much earlier, even doing this before castling, making a way for the pawns to by-pass the pieces in their advance.

This objective is so patent that it does not require elucidation by master games. We shall illustrate it in another connexion.

5. Formation of pieces to achieve the pawn storm

In an earlier example (Diagram 5, Konstantinopolsky–Frank), it was in fact Black who struck the first blow in the pawn attack, in an attack which however he could not follow up. The reason for this was that his pawns were badly placed and could not reinforce the attack in time. It is therefore of importance that when a pawn storm is set in motion, in addition to other factors, one should also pay attention to the power of one's own pieces to provide help for the pawn storm.

The position below is quoted from the game Kotov–Poliak in the Moscow–Ukraine match, 1937.

Poliak

12

Kotov

It is clear both sides are thinking about commencing an attack on the King. Superficially it seems that everything speaks in favour of Black's attack succeeding. Black has the opportunity of speedily fastening on to the White pawn on QR3 and of opening up the QKt file once the pawn from QKt3 has reached QKt5. This in fact is what actually happens. Black enjoys success with his offensive at the beginning, but the continuation shows that White has seen further ahead. Eventually it becomes clear that the Black pieces cannot help in bringing the pawn storm to a successful conclusion.

It is on the contrary White who has accurately worked out his pawn storm as a combination and who first succeeds in seizing the initiative. His pieces cooperate in the action and arrive just at the right time on the field of battle where they consummate the attack that the infantry has prepared.

1.	P – KKt4	Q – Kt2
2.	P – KR4	P – QKt4
3.	Q – Q3!	

One of the moves of a series that has been worked out before-hand. White aims at a speedy march with the KRP to R6. Thereafter Black cannot prevent the opening up of lines, since in reply to P – Kt3 there would follow the Knight sacrifice on Kt6. At the same time White prevents the move P – Kt5 since P – QR4 then follows, after which P – Kt6 is impossible. Such a move, uniting attack on one wing with defence on the other side of the board, is very effective in games where both sides have wing attacks.

3.	....	Kt – K1

Black does not defend himself in the best way. By driving away the Knight from White's KB4 with B – Q3 Poliak could have substantially defended his position against White's attack. But now he incurs great difficulties.

4.	P – R5	R – B3
5.	P – Kt5	R – Q3
6.	Q – B5	P – Kt5
7.	P × P	P – R4

Black has in fact been able to open up lines, in some measure at any rate. But White's pieces exert a decisive pressure.

8.	P – Kt6	Kt – B3
9.	P – R6!	

Poliak

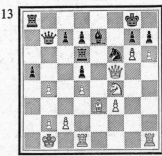

13

Kotov

A colourful-looking position. White's pawns have flung themselves bodily on to the enemy bayonets. Their endeavours meet with energetic assistance on the part of the remaining White pieces.

| 9. .... | P × KKtP |
| 10. Q × KtP | B – B1 |

Or 10. Kt – K1; 11. P – R7 ch, K – R1; 12. Q × R, and 13. Kt – Kt6 mate.

| 11. P – R7 ch | Kt × P |

And 11. .... K – R1 also loses: 12. Q – B7, Kt × P; 13. R × Kt ch, K × R; 14. R – R1 ch, R – R3; 15. R × R ch, K × R; 16. Q – Kt6 mate.

12. Q × Kt ch	K – B2
13. Q – B5 ch	K – Kt1
14. Kt – Kt6	R – KB3
15. R – R8 ch	K – B2
16. Kt – K5 ch	K – K1
17. Q × P mate.	

We have now studied a number of examples of pawn storms when castling takes place on opposite sides. In all cases both White and Black have carried out pawn attacks on the side where their own King is not placed. Thus the pawns have been able to advance boldly without the King becoming exposed. But there does exist an exceptional case. In some games the players suddenly begin to behave in a manner quite the opposite to that dictated by sound judgement. They advance their pawns, not on the wing opposite to that where their own King is placed, but, on the contrary, just in front of their own King! However, such a strategy may be right in some cases and it is employed above all when the centre is closed. This often occurs, in particular in the Samisch variation of the King's Indian Defence. We shall now consider such a case.

Szabo

14

Kotov

The position in the diagram arose in a game Kotov–Szabo (Candidates' Tournament, Zurich, 1953). The players have castled on opposite sides. Their respective plans of campaign seem obvious: White's offensive on the King's wing, Black's on the Queen's wing. But this is too superficial a consideration. Black has an exceptionally strong position on the King's wing and the same remark is valid about White's defensive resources on the Queen's wing. And so the opponents exchange places; White begins his attack on the left side of the board and Black rushes in with his pawn storm on the other side where one cannot catch even a glimpse of the White King.

| 1. .... | P – Kt4! |

A pawn offensive of this type is possible where there is a completely blocked centre.

2. P – KR3	Kt – B3
3. Kt – Kt5	P – R4
4. R – R1!	

Attack on one flank must be combined with defensive on the other. On R1 the Rook fulfils an important defensive task.

4.	R – KR2
5. R – B3	P – Kt5
6. RP × P	P × P
7. R – QR3	B – Kt6
8. R × R	Q × R
9. Kt – B1 !	

With the intention of capturing on QR5, a move that would be bad at once since Black can recapture on R5 and give check with the Queen on KR8.

9	Q – R8 !

A bold counter-attack. Now there ensues a phase with interesting combinational turns during which the game attains a high climax.

10. Kt × BP	P × P
11. P × P	R – R2
12. Kt – K6	

From this menacing post the Knight will be able to direct a decisive blow against the enemy King.

12.	B – K8
13. Q – Q1	R – R2
14. R – Q3	R – R7
15. P – R3	Kt – Q2
16. Q – R4	Q – Kt7
17. R – Kt3	B – B6 !

A very pretty counter-stroke ! After 18. Q × Kt, Black wins by a combination on a well-known theme : 18. .... Q × P ch ; 19. R × Q, R × R ch ; 20. K – R1, R – Kt2 dis ch and 21. .... R × Q. But now there follows a tactical counter-thrust.

18. Kt – K2 !	

A pretty finishing stroke. If the Queen captures the Knight then White wins by 19. R – Kt8 ch, Kt × R ; 20. Q – K8 ch, followed by mate. Hence Szabo resigned at once. The final position deserves a diagram.

Szabo

Kotov

In conclusion, we have a few more remarks to make. We have now examined the pawn storm as the principal method to be used in positions where castling takes place on opposite sides. But it happens, and very often too in master practice, that the attack is carried out not with the help of pawns but by means of pieces. The game runs in this latter way when the players have castled on the same side. In positions of opposite-side castling, even though a piece attack may seem to present the most plausible continuation, none the less a pawn attack will prove to be preferable. Anyone who wishes to learn how to play chess well must make himself or herself thoroughly conversant with the play in positions where the players have castled on opposite sides. For this purpose it is especially profitable to play through a whole series of games in which one has come to a prior agreement with the opponent to castle opposite sides. Such practice teaches a beginner how to master the principles of the struggle and to acquire the knack of the difficult play that occurs when both sides attack with pawns.

ATTACK ON SAME-SIDE CASTLED POSITIONS

In a very great number of games both players castle on the same side, most frequently on the King's side. Here the play can be conducted both in the centre and on the wings. An important role in this connexion is played by the pawn formation that arises in the centre after the opening. The flank attack may be either directed against the King or else it may take place on the Queen's wing. We shall now consider cases of attack on the King when both Kings are positioned on the same side of the board.

How should one set about the attack on the King? Perhaps by hurling forward the pawns in the same fashion as in opposite-side castling? As we have already seen, this too is a possible method of attack, but special positional conditions are required for it. For the most part the attack on the King in positions where players have castled on the same side is made with the aid of the pieces and the pawns play only a contributory role.

Naturally, the attacker seeks to increase his pressure against the enemy King's position to the maximum extent so as to be able to carry out a successful direct mating attack, and if that is not practicable he tries to attain a material advantage so great as to be sufficient for the win. This is not so simple. Between the attacking pieces and the King there stand the defending pieces and pawns. What shall one do with them and how can one get them out of the way?

It is a comparatively simple matter as far as the pieces are concerned. Under the increasing pressure the opponent is forced either to remove them, or else to submit to their exchange. Removing the pieces that defend the approaches to the King naturally allows a decisive attack. The matter is considerably more complicated when it relates to pawns that protect the King. They are 'steadfast till death', and cannot just retire. One must therefore either remove them from one's path or else force them to advance: either break through the pawn shield of the King; or else weaken it so that in both cases the attacking pieces can set in motion a decisive assault.

This is the entire process of the attack. Depending on how one deals with the pawn shield of the King, one can distinguish between the following methods of attack.

1. The pawn storm. A risky method of attack which one rarely encounters. It is only possible when the centre is solidly closed.

2. Demolition of the enemy King-side pawn position by a piece sacrifice. Sometimes too, attacking pawns can perform a service in this blasting process. In the blasting operation the attacking pieces come into immediate contact with the opponent's pieces, and seek to beat them down in hand-to-hand combat.

3. *Weakening the pawn shield.* The attacking pieces force the opponent's pawns to advance and thereby open up a way for the attacking combat troops. Black's pawns stand, for instance, on KB2, KKt2, and KR2. White exerts pressure on the points Kt2 and R2 and forces the move P – KKt3. Then the diagonal KR1 – QR8 becomes weak, and along this line the White pieces can arrive at KKt7 and KR8. In addition, KR3 and KB3 become weak squares. The attacker has attained his goal.

4. *Opening lines and diagonals.* The attacker opens up a line or a diagonal and settles himself down to lasting possession of it. Eventually the attacking pieces utilize this as a connecting link from which to break into the opponent's position.

5. *By-passing manoeuvres (switching the attack from the centre to a flank).* The pieces approach the opponent's King after having taken a long, roundabout way through the centre (or via the Queen's wing, according to circumstance).

Now we shall go through all the attacking methods given above to explain the different strategic and tactical characteristics in each case.

1. The pawn storm

A pawn storm where both players have castled on the same side is only possible when the centre is securely locked. When one plans a pawn offensive on the King's wing one must bear in mind the most important strategic rule in chess: *a counter-thrust in the centre is the best reply to a wing attack.* In addition one must see to it that the defending pieces cannot take the attacking pieces in the flank or direct a decisive attack from the flank after one has made some weakening pawn moves in front of one's own King.

We shall now go through the most important types of pawn storms.

Kan

16

Riumin

The diagram position arose in the game Riumin–Kan (from the 1936 International Tournament, in Moscow). The centre is comparatively stable and hence Riumin decides to set in motion a pawn offensive on the King's wing. It is true that in the meantime Black will gain possession of the open K file but White has cleverly worked out that Black cannot undertake any dangerous enterprise along this file.

So the play developed as follows:

1.	P – B4	P – B3
2.	B × B	Q × B
3.	R – B3	B – K3
4.	K – R1	R – K2
5.	R – KKt1	QR – K1
6.	P – KKt4 !	

All preparatory measures have been taken and now White's pawns commence the storming of the enemy position.

6.	....	B – B2
7.	Q – B2	K – R1
8.	P – KR4	P – QR3?

Kan forgets the principle we have just formulated. By means of the counter-thrust in the centre, P – QB4, he could have posed great difficulties to his opponent. Now White's attack is free to develop without hindrance.

54

9.	P – B5	P – B4

This advance now comes too late.

10.	Kt – K2	P × P
11.	P × P	Q – Kt5

In the hope of weakening the pressure from White's pieces by means of an exchange of Rooks. But Riumin demonstrates that his attack is not to be withstood.

12.	Kt – B4	R – K8
13.	R – Kt3	R × R ch
14.	R × R	Q – K2
15.	P – Kt5	P × P
16.	P × P	Q – K6

An interesting moment. Black perceives that the pawn offensive is becoming critically dangerous and tries to force an exchange of Queens. But the end game is won for White after this exchange. It happens so often in just this way that the end result of even the most violent attack turns out to be 'merely' a won ending.

17.	Q × Q	R × Q
18.	K – Kt2	B – K1
19.	K – B2	R – K2
20.	R – QB1	B – B3
21.	K – B3	R – KB2
22.	K – Kt4	

Kan

Riumin

Now *23.* B × P is threatened. It is becoming more and more difficult for Black to defend his position.

| 22. .... | R – B2 |
| 23. Kt – K6 | Kt × Kt |

Also after *23.* .... R – B1, Black's plight would be hopeless.

24. P × Kt	K – Kt1
25. K – B5	K – B1
26. K – K5	

The position of White's King in the centre together with the strong advanced pawn on K6 decide the game.

26.	P – KKt3
27. K – Q6	R – K2
28. B × RP	K – K1
29. B – Q3	Black resigns.

Here is yet another example of a pawn storm, carried out in a position that is advantageous for White in view of all the positional factors involved.

The diagram position arose in a game Alekhine–Monticelli (San Remo, 1930). The centre is closed. As yet White's piece attack has had no success to speak of.

After a thorough consideration of the character of the position Alekhine throws his pawns on the King's side into the struggle.

Monticelli

Alekhine

1. P – Kt4!

At just the right moment. Now Black cannot play *1.* P × Kt on account of *2.* P × B, Q × P; *3.* R × Kt.

1.	B – Kt3
2. Kt – B3	Kt – Q1
3. Kt – K1	

An interesting regrouping. The Knight which just now stood in such a menacing position disappears deep behind the front line so as to yield place to the infantry.

3.	P – QB3
4. Kt – Q3	Kt – K3
5. P – KB4!	

White's pawns constitute by themselves a powerful attack against which Monticelli must undertake the most exceptional measures.

5.	P – KB4
6. P × P e.p.	B × P
7. P – B5	Kt × P
8. P × Kt	B × P ch

Naturally, the piece sacrifice weakens the pressure of White's pawns, but the compensation Black receives for the Knight is obviously insufficient and Alekhine is able to exploit his material superiority in convincing style.

9. K – Kt2	QR – K1
10. Q – B3	B – B2
11. Kt – B4	B – K4
12. B – R3	R – KKt1
13. B – B5	B – Kt1
14. B – KB2	R – K5?
15. Q × R	resigns.

A pawn offensive in front of one's own castled position is very risky. We have already touched upon this in a couple of examples. Now we shall see what calamities a defectively motivated pawn storm can entail.

The next diagram position is from a game Capablanca–Ilyin-Genevsky which has become regarded as classical on account of the outstandingly elegant play achieved by the Leningrad master.

Ilyin-Genevsky

19

Capablanca

Since the centre is not closed the opportunity exists for some very brisk skirmishes in the central squares. Nevertheless Capablanca sets into motion a pawn attack on the King's wing. 'Where does that leave us then?' the surprised reader may perhaps ask. 'Doesn't the World Champion, with his marvellous intuition of chess strategy, understand the elementary principles?'

Naturally Capablanca is acquainted with these precepts; but here he manifestly underestimates an unknown chess-master. 'For me, everything is possible' – this idea surely must have dominated the Cuban when he embarked on his pawn attack.

1. P – KKt4	KR – Q1
2. P – KB4	B – K1!

Genevsky defends himself remarkably well. His Knight on KB3 is to be transferred to KB1, from where it will defend the point KR2, and the Bishop stands on K1 so as to protect the KB2 square. Black has determined to meet the pawn storm threatened by the World Champion with rock-like dourness.

3.	P – Kt5	Kt – Q2
4.	P – B5	P – Kt4
5.	Kt – B4	P – Kt5

Having first set up his lines of defence Genevsky starts on a pawn attack on the other wing without a moment's delay. The QKt file which is now opened up performs excellent service as a communication line for the Black pieces when they endeavour to strike out on the Queen's wing, or in the centre or even against the White King.

6.	P – B6	B – B1

A cool defence. After 6. .... KP × P; 7. Kt – Q5, White's threats would become really dangerous.

7.	Kt – B2	KtP × P
8.	KtP × P	P – K3 !

Now the points KB2 and KKt2 are securely protected. There remains one weak point – KR2 – and Capablanca at once hastens to attack it.

9.	P – KR4	

It seems as though White has a comfortable winning method: the opening up of the KR file and then the mating attack along the open file. But it turns out that things do not go so easily for him as Genevsky's counter-attack strikes at precisely the right moment.

9.	....	R – Kt1 !
10.	P – R5	R – Kt3
11.	P × P	RP × P
12.	Kt – Q1	

White is preparing to transfer his Queen to the King's wing, but, before he does this, the points QKt2 and QB3 must be protected.

12.	....	Kt(Q2) – K4
13.	Q – KB2	Kt – KKt5
14.	Q – R4	Kt(B3) – K4 !

Black conducts the defence in excellent style. After *14. ....*
Kt × B; *15.* Kt × Kt, Q × BP White would play *16.* Kt – Kt4,
with the fruitful threat of Kt – R6 ch.

15.	P – Q4	Kt × B
16.	Kt × Kt	Q × BP
17.	P × Kt	Q × Kt ch
18.	K – R1?	

After the game long and deep analysis showed that White
should rather have retired his King to R2 in order to retain
some attacking chances. Now, however, White's position falls
to pieces.

18.	....	P × P
19.	R – B3	

Up to here Capablanca has reckoned it all out. But a remarkable surprise awaits him.

Ilyin-Genevsky

20

Capablanca

19.	....	P × Kt!

A Queen sacrifice. In compensation Black obtains a Rook,
Bishop, and pawn, but, most important of all, he can set into
motion an especially powerful counter-attack.

20.	R × Q	P × R
21.	Q – K1	

Or *21*. R – K1, R – Kt7; *22*. R × P, R – Q8 ch; *23*. K – R2, R(Q8) – Q7 with decisive advantage for Black.

21.	R – Kt7
22. Q × P	R(Q1) – Q7
23. B – B3	P – B5
24. P – R3	B – Q3
25. Q – R7	

Or *25*. P – K5, B – B2 and the Bishop exerts a decisive effect along the diagonal QR2 – KKt8.

25.	P – B6
White resigns.	

The next example shows with classical simplicity how Black can be punished for sinning against elementary strategic principles. Without having first secured his central position Maroczy suddenly starts a pawn march on the King's wing. Alekhine carries out a counter-thrust in the centre whereupon Black's whole position falls to pieces at one fell swoop.

In this game (from the tournament at Carlsbad, 1923) Maroczy suddenly decides to commence a pawn attack on White's King's side.

Maroczy

Alekhine

1.	P – KKt4

This plan is obviously faulty. The centre is far from closed and White can easily institute a counter-thrust there. But just observe how precisely Alekhine achieves it!

2.	Kt – Q2!	R – B2
3.	P – B3	P – K4

Even without this fresh weakening of his position Black would have stood quite badly. He cannot prevent White's decisive P – K4.

4.	P × QP	BP × P
5.	P – K4!	BP × P
6.	BP × P	R × R ch
7.	R × R	KP × P
8.	Q – B7!	

This annihilates Black's last hope – 8. Q × P, Q – B4; with a Queen exchange. The energetic sally with the Queen fetters all Black's pieces and presages an immediate catastrophe.

8.	. . . .	K – Kt2
9.	R – B5	P × P
10.	Kt × P	Q – Kt5
11.	R × P ch	resigns.

Let us now summarize all that has been said about the pawn storm in positions with castling on the same side. This can only rightfully take place when and when only the centre is completely closed. One must weigh up and reckon out exactly whether the opponent can break open the centre and thereby organize some counter-play of significance. Should such be the case one must at once banish all thoughts of such an attack from one's mind, and instead try to carry out the offensive against the opponent's King only with the help of the pieces, or, if need be, by flinging in one or more pawns into the assault.

When we can ascertain for sure that the opponent has not the opportunity of breaking open the centre or of making a noticeable counter-thrust in the centre, then we can undertake a pawn storm without hesitation. In such circumstances it can indeed be of great effect.

2. *Demolition of the enemy King-side pawn position by a piece sacrifice*

Here you weaken or lay bare the opponent's King by the aid of the piece sacrifice. The process entails the surrender of an attacking piece for an enemy pawn, or else the capture of the pawn itself, with the result that the King's position is opened up, thereby giving direct access to the attacking pieces.

The diagram position below occurred in a game between Kotov and Bronstein (Thirteenth U.S.S.R. Championship, 1945). Black's King is more or less protected by its own pawns. The ensuing Knight sacrifice makes it possible for White to smash all the enemy bulwarks to smithereens and to finish off the offensive with a mating attack.

Bronstein

Kotov

1. Kt × BP!

The Knight is sacrificed for two pawns, after which the remaining White pieces obtain many open lines and diagonals.

| *1.* .... | R × Kt |
| *2.* Kt × P! | |

This is stronger than *2.* B × KP, R × B; *3.* P × R, P × P.

| *2.* .... | Q – B1 |
| *3.* Kt – Q6 | R × B |

Accelerating the loss. He could have put up a longer resistance by *3*. . . . . P × B; *4*. Kt × R, P × P; *5*. Kt × B, P – B6; *6*. R – KB1, Q – B4 ch.

4.	P × R	P × P
5.	R – KB1	Q – K2
6.	Kt – B5	Q – B4 ch
7.	K – R1	Kt – B3
8.	Kt × B	Kt(K4) – Kt5

Black develops his pieces and at the same time sets an insidious trap. If now *8*. Q – Q8 ch, K × Kt; *9*. P – KR3, then there would follow *9*. . . . . Kt – B7 ch; *10*. K – R2, B × P; *11*. Q × R, Kt(B3) – Kt5 ch; *12*. K – Kt1, Kt – K5 dis ch; *13*. K – R1, Kt × P mate.

9. R × Kt!

White avoids, just in time, the outspread net.

9.	. . . .	K × Kt
10.	R – KB1	B – K3
11.	Q – K2	R – R1
12.	P – KR3	Kt – K6
13.	P – QKt4	Q – K4
14.	QR – K1	resigns.

And here is yet another example on the same theme from a game Allegat–Alekhine (Paris, 1914).

Alekhine

Allegat

White's position seems to be absolutely safe. The Knight must quit R4 and then no threat hangs over White's head, or so it seems. But on the contrary it turns out that White stands badly.

The brilliant piece sacrifice that now follows lays bare at one blow the whole of White's King's wing and provides Alekhine's pieces with opportunities for developing a fierce attack.

1.	B × P!
2. P × B	P – B6

This fresh sacrifice reveals the deep import of Alekhine's plan.

3. R × P

Nor are other continuations of any avail, e.g.:

(1) *3.* Q – K3, Q × P ch; *4.* K – R1, B – R5; *5.* B – Q2 (the Rook cannot leave B2 on account of *5.* .... P – B7 with mate on Kt8), *5.* .... Kt – B5; *6.* Q × KBP, Kt × B! and Black wins easily;

(2) *3.* Q – Q1, Q × P ch; *4.* K – R1, B – R5; *5.* Kt – K3, Q – R6; *6.* B – B1, Kt – Kt6 ch; *7.* K – Kt1, Kt × B; *8.* Q × Kt, B × R ch; *9.* Q × B, R – B5! and Black's attack is not to be checked;

(3) *3.* Q – B2! The best move. *3.* .... Q × P ch; *4.* K – R1, B – R5; *5.* Kt – K3, Q – R6; *6.* B – B1, Kt – Kt6 ch; *7.* K – Kt1, Kt × B; *8.* Kt × Kt, B × R ch; *9.* Q × B, Q – Kt5 ch; *10.* Kt – Kt3, P – KR4! and Black should win.

3.	Q × P ch
4. R – Kt3	R × Kt ch!

Yet another thunderbolt of a combination. The White King is entirely deprived of protection.

5. K × R	Kt × R ch
6. P × Kt	Q × KtP
7. Q – K3	R – B1 ch
8. K – K2	Q – Kt5 ch

White resigns.

The inevitable 9. .... B – Kt4 (either at once or else after a check on R5) decides the game.

3. Weakening the pawn shield

This method of attack is simple and easy to understand. By continually increasing the pressure of the pieces on the opponent's King's position we compel him to advance one of the pawns that protect the King. This occasions the weakening of the King-side defence by virtue of a breach through which the attacking pieces can penetrate. Sometimes it is a matter of breaking down the pawn shield after one has exchanged or captured some of the pawns. Then the weaknesses in the defensive bulwarks become especially noticeable and the attack is the most effective.

We append an example. This position arose in the game Kotov–Lissitzin (Eleventh U.S.S.R. Championship, 1939). Black has been interested only in operations on the Queen's wing and has neglected White's attack against the King. In the ensuing phase of the game White's energetic play gives him the opportunity of setting into motion a powerful attack against the weak points on Black's King's side.

Lissitzin

Kotov

1. B × Kt	Kt × B
2. Kt – B5 !	

66

The first weakness has been localized – the KKt7 square. The Knight is directed against it and the White Queen is also ready to attack it from the KKt5 square.

    2. ....   R – K4

Neither this nor any other defensive move saves Black. After 2. .... Kt × P there follows 3. R × Kt, R × R; 4. Q – Kt5, P – Kt3; 5. Q – B6. Bad also is 2. .... Q × P; 3. Q – Kt5, Kt – R4; 4. R – B1, and 5. Q × Kt.

It is easy to convince oneself that no other defensive means can avert the catastrophe on the weak point KKt7.

    3. Kt × QP

The Rook move has given some support to Black's KKt2. White answers by changing the centre of gravity of the attack, concentrating on the point KB7.

    3. ....   Q × P
    4. Q – B4   P – Q6
    5. R – K3

The strongest move. If 5. Kt × P then 5. .... R(Kt1) – K1; 6. Kt – Q6 dis ch, K – R1 and Black has retained the dangerous passed pawn on Q6.

    5. ....   B – B7
    6. Kt × P   R(K5) – K1

Black has not seen his opponent's deadly threat on the eighth move. Better would have been 6. .... Q × B, but also then 7. Kt × R, Q – Kt4; 8. Kt × P would have given White sufficient advantage for the win.

    7. P – K5   Q – Q5
    8. Q – Kt5!

Black had not reckoned with this move. White's pieces once again become interested in the weak point on KKt7. Now Black loses equally by 8. .... Kt – Q4; 9. Kt – R6 ch, and 10. Kt – B5, as well as by 8. .... P – Q7; 9. P × Kt, Q × P; 10. R × R ch, R × R; 11. Q × QP.

8.	Q × B
9. Kt – R6 ch	K – B1
10. P × Kt	P – Kt3
11. Kt – B5	Q – B2
12. Kt – Q6	R × R
13. Q – R6 ch	K – Kt1
14. Kt × Q	K × Kt
15. P × R	K – K3
16. P – B7	resigns.

4. Opening lines and diagonals

This method of attack does not need much recommendation. How often in fact has not the Black King been checkmated along the diagonal QR1 – KR8 or along QKt1 – KR7. We will give only one example on this theme.

The diagram position is taken from a game Averbakh–Panno in the match Argentine–U.S.S.R. at Buenos Aires, 1954.

Panno

Averbakh

The centre being closed, the play takes place on the flanks. Averbakh, who has left his own King's position untouched, hastens to initiate an attack on the King's wing.

1. P – KKt4	Kt – K1
2. P – R4	P – B4
3. P – R5	P – B5
4. P – Kt5	

Here we have one example of the pawn storm. In this case it is absolutely safe for White as the centre is closed and there is no counter-threat.

4.		R – B2
5. B – Kt4		Q – Q1

Or 5. .... B × B; 6. Q × B, Q – Kt5; 7. P × P, P × P; 8. Q – B8, R – K2; 9. P – Kt3, and White's attack is very dangerous.

6. B × B		Q × B
7. Kt – B3		B – B1
8. K – K2		R – Kt2
9. R – R4		Kt – Q2
10. P × P		P × P

An important line has been opened up on the King's side, and Averbakh at once throws all his major pieces into the breach.

11. Q – R1		B – K2
12. R – R8 ch		K – B2
13. Q – R6		Kt – B1
14. R – R1		R – QKt1

Panno

26

Averbakh

15. B × P!

A characteristic sacrifice. White is in complete control of the open file, and, by the aid of a sacrifice, broadens the base of operations for his pieces.

| 15. .... | Q – B2 |

If *15. .... P × B*; then *16. R – R4*.

16. Q – R2	Kt – Q2
17. Q – R3	Kt – B1
18. R × Kt ch!	

This leads quickest to the desired goal. Otherwise White would have taken a long time to win, despite having an extra pawn and the superior position.

18.	K × R
19. Q – K6	R – Kt1
20. Kt – R4	B – Q1
21. Kt × P ch	K – Kt2

Or *21. .... R × Kt*; *22. R – R8 ch*, K – Kt2; *23. Q – Kt8* mate.

| 22. Kt × P | resigns. |

5. *By-passing manoeuvres (switching the attack from the centre to a flank)*

This often arises when the attack in the game has commenced either on the centre or on the Queen's side. As the struggle develops so the operations are transferred to the King's wing. In this way the attacking pieces approach the King in an indirect manner.

Smyslov

27

Ravinsky

Here is a remarkable example on the theme. The diagram shows a position from the game Ravinsky–Smyslov (Moscow Championship, 1944). White controls more space and his pieces display greater activity. But Smyslov embarks on a deeply thought out counter-attack on the Queen's wing and the influence of this expands over the whole board.

1.	P – QKt3!

Preparing freedom of movement for the Black pieces, in particular for the Bishop.

2. R – QB1	P – B4!
3. QP × P	B × Kt

An adequate solution of the problem of the position. Black relinquishes the two Bishops in order to increase the degree of activity of the other pieces.

4. Q × B	P × P
5. B – B1	Q – Kt3
6. P – Kt5	`

An attempt at thwarting, to some extent at any rate, Black's initiative on the Queen's wing. But it is already too late and Smyslov seizes hold of the play in a merciless grip.

6.	P – B5!

The pawn is not to be captured on account of 7. .... Kt – Kt5!

7. P – R3	P – B6
8. Q – Kt3	B – B4
9. R – B2	

Now there comes the decisive move. But no better would have been 9. R – K2, e.g. 9. .... B × P ch; 10. R × B, Kt × P; 11. R – B2, Kt × R and 12. .... P – B7.

9.	R – Q7!
10. R × R	P × R
11. R – K2	B × P ch

Remarkable accomplishment of Black's strategy. His pieces come closer and closer to the White King.

12.	K – Kt2	R – B6 !
13.	Q – Q1	B – K6
14.	Kt × P	Q – Q5
15.	Q – K1	Kt × P

Smyslov

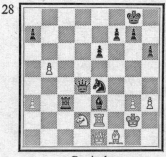

28

Ravinsky

An interesting metamorphosis of the position is to be seen here. The counter-attack that was commenced on the Queen's wing first changed over to the centre and thereafter was directed against the White King. Now Black finishes off the struggle by an energetic pursuit of the weakened and vulnerable White King.

16.	Kt × Kt	Q × Kt ch
17.	K – R2	Q – Q5

With the deadly threat of *18.* . . . . R – B8.

18.	R – KKt2	R – B8
19.	Q – K2	Q – R8
20.	Q × B	R × B
21.	P – Kt4	R – K8

White resigns.

72

ATTACK AGAINST THE UNCASTLED KING

In the opening both players endeavour to develop their pieces, to occupy the central squares, and to remove their King to the flanks where it stands more protected.

Naturally, it is to one's advantage if the opponent cannot solve all these opening problems. It is of course always advantageous to keep the opponent's pieces on their original squares as long as possible when they cannot obtain control of master points in the centre, and, in particular, when the enemy King has not succeeded in tucking itself away in safety. A King that is left standing in the centre is an ideal object of attack, and it is worth a great deal to attain such an objective. Therefore masters will often use every possible means available to keep the opponent's King right in the middle of the board. It is well worth while. When the King stands just on its original square one can, as has already been said, expose it to a fierce attack, and therefore masters sometimes sacrifice both pawns and pieces solely to prevent the opponent's castling.

See for example how Paul Keres sacrifices in the following game against Sajtar in the Chess Olympiad at Amsterdam, 1954.

Sajtar

29

Keres

1. B × KP!

This sacrifice does not lead inevitably to mate, but it deprives Black of the right to castle.

1.	P × B
2. Kt × P	Q – B5

Even worse would be 2. .... Q – Kt1; 3. Kt – Q5, Kt × Kt; 4. P × Kt, or 3. .... K – B2; 4. B × Kt, Kt × B; 5. Kt – Kt5 ch.

3. Kt – Q5	K – B2

So Black has now definitively relinquished the right to castle. This defenceless wanderer in the centre is doomed to a long and difficult existence there.

4. B × Kt	K × Kt

If 4. .... Kt × B; then 5. Kt – Kt5 ch and White's attack is too dangerous. Nevertheless, this would have been best, since now White can force the ensuing moves.

5. B – B3 !	

The intention is, after 5. .... K – B2, to give Black short shrift with 6. Q – R5 ch, P – Kt3; 7. Q – B3 ch, K – Kt1; 8. Kt – B6 ch.

5.	Kt – B3
6. B × Kt	P × B
7. Kt – Kt6	Q – B3
8. Kt × R	

'All roads lead to Rome' in this position. Also 8. Q – Q5 ch,, would win.

8.	B – K2
9. P – QR4	P – QKt3
10. Q – Q5 ch	K – Q2
11. R – R3	B – Q1
12. Kt × P ch!	resigns.

There are many other examples that could be quoted to show how the attacker sacrifices a piece for one or two pawns with the sole aim of keeping the opponent's King right in the middle of the first rank. I can, for instance, cite a remarkable telephone game between Bengt Horberg and myself.

After Black's ninth move this position arose.

Kotov

30

Horberg

By *10. Kt – Q5!* Horberg sacrificed a piece for two pawns. I thought that White's attack could be warded off, but my adversary's subtle play, resourceful and imaginative, enabled him to bring the whole combination to a successful conclusion.

Now let us take up an important question. What plan ought we to decide upon when the opponent's King is pinned down to the middle of the board?

We can take as our point of departure a position in which our pieces are practically fully developed, castling has been carried out, and many of our opponent's pieces in fact stand on their original squares. So now we have his King stuck fast in the centre. How shall we set about it, what sort of plan shall we fashion as our continuation?

The answer to these questions soon comes to mind. When we have the better development and our pieces display more activity, then these circumstances must be exploited at once. We are in effect obliged to set about harassing the opponent without loss of time by direct threats and swift attacks. He must be forced to ward off these attacks at once. This has the specific effect of hindering him still further from completing the development of his pieces. Finally, the attack should attain such overwhelming force as to bring about the win for us.

We shall examine an instructive game on this theme. It was played between Kotov and Kalmanok at Moscow in 1935.

French Defence

WHITE: KOTOV	BLACK: KALMANOK
1. P – Q4	P – K3
2. P – K4	P – Q4
3. Kt – QB3	Kt – KB3
4. B – Kt5	P × P
5. Kt × P	B – K2
6. B × Kt	P × B
7. Kt – KB3	Kt – Q2
8. B – B4!	

Black has adopted a slow opening system with the result that he remains backward in development. This Bishop move lessens the power of movement of the Black pieces still more, since after the natural P – QB4 there would follow P – Q5.

8.	P – B3
9. Q – Q2	P – Kt3

Kalmanok

31

Kotov

76

Let us pause and consider this position for a moment. White has brought out nearly all his pieces whereas Black obviously stands badly as regards his development. But if White delays for one or two moves – if, in other words, he puts off for a time the decisive operations – then Black too will be able to complete the development of his pieces and castle.

But White does not delay the attack and instead at once initiates a decisive offensive against the enemy position.

10. Q – R6!

This move has as its temporary aim 11. Q – Kt7, winning the KRP. It forces Black to make yet another move with a piece that has already been developed.

10.		B – B1
11. Q – B4		B – QKt2
12. O – O – O		P – KR4
13. K – Kt1		B – K2
14. Q – Kt3!		

The same strategy again! This threatens 15. Q – Kt7 and 16. Q – R7, when the KRP would fall. Defensive measures must once again be taken.

14.		Kt – B1
15. KR – K1		P – KB4

White has developed his pieces rapidly, while the Black King still stands in the middle of the board. It is therefore hardly surprising that the pretty move that now follows should decide the whole game.

16. P – Q5!   BP × P

He cannot play 16. .... KP × P because of 17. Kt – B6 mate, while if 16. .... P × Kt; then 17. P × KP, followed by P × P ch.

17. B – Kt5 ch		Kt – Q2
18. Kt – K5		Q – B2

Black has given up the ghost. Retreat of the QB leads to a pleasant mate after *18.* .... B – QB1; *19.* Q – Kt7, R – B1; *20.* R × P!, P × R; *21.* Kt – B6 ch, B × Kt; *22.* Kt – Kt6 dis ch, B – K2; *23.* Q × R.

19. B × Kt ch	K – Q1
20. Q – Kt7	R – KB1
21. Kt – Kt5	Q – B4
22. B × P	resigns.

We will conclude this chapter on the attack on the King with a remarkable example, signed Alekhine, that unparalleled master among attacking players. His game with Veillat is of supreme interest by reason of the way the attack is built up, and it can serve as a copybook example *par excellence* of our theme.

Alekhine

32

Veillat

In the diagram position Black is ahead in development. White requires two more moves before his King can gain the haven of KKt1. In the meantime Alekhine creates positive threats so that his opponent is not in a position to make just the two moves that are necessary to complete his development.

1.	Q – R6!

The pawn on QR2 must be protected.

2. R – B2	R – Q1
3. R – Q2	

3. Q – B1, would be bad on account of Kt – Kt5!

3.	B – Kt5
4. B – K2	R × R
5. Kt × R	

Also after *5.* Q × R, R – Q1, White would inevitably lose.

5.	B × B
6. Q – R1 ch!	

An excellent defensive move. The pawn on QR2 is saved but soon the threatening thundercloud returns to hang over the White King.

6.	P – B3
7. K × B	Q – R3 ch
8. Kt – B4	P – QKt4
9. Kt – Kt2	P – Kt5 dis ch
10. K – K1	

Or *10.* Kt – B4, Kt – R4; *11.* R – QB1, R – QB1 and White loses a pawn.

10.	R – QB1
11. P – B3	Kt – Q5!

A brilliant finishing stroke. The Black Rook penetrates via QB7 and this signifies the inevitable end.

12. P × Kt	R – B7
13. Kt – B4	

Another way of incurring a complete collapse was by *13.* Q – Q1, R × Kt.

13.	Q – K3 ch
14. Kt – K5	P × Kt
15. K – Q1	Q – B4
resigns.	

3

HOW TO DEFEND DIFFICULT POSITIONS

P. Keres

Questions concerning attack or defence are the most important
in chess; they are as old as the game itself and probably canno[t]
all be answered objectively. Many players want to attack all th[e]
time and to attain the win by overpowering the opponent'[s]
fighting forces. Others, on the contrary, build up their positio[n]
as surely as possible, as if to say – just come on, I am ready
for you. Each player has his own inclinations and according t[o]
these inclinations he sets out his game.

It is clear that the attacking player always leaves a bigge[r]
impression on the general public. Beautiful sacrificial combina[-]
tions, surprising continuations, bold attacks, and brilliant mat[-]
ing play are always more attractive to amateurs than any kin[d]
of defensive achievement. One may conduct a game to a wi[n]
through logical play and deeply thought-out defence, but suc[h]
a game can never be so popular as a successful surprise win.
Thus, and there is no doubt about this, the general preferenc[e]
(and perhaps with some justice) favours the notion that th[e]
basic idea in the game of chess is in fact an attack on th[e]
opponent's King.

Despite this one should not underestimate the importance o[f]
a good defence. When one studies games from the previou[s]
century one notices in general a colossal over-estimation of th[e]
attack. Most of the time everybody tried only to give mate, an[d]
if a promising attack was obtained then the win was as good a[s]
assured. Defensive play was deemed tedious and in consequenc[e]
it was but little developed. Only towards the end of the nine[-]
teenth century did some masters point out how over-estimate[d]
a role the attack was playing and then acquire for themselve[s]
a good defensive technique. Among these one must single ou[t]
in the first place the world champions Steinitz and Lasker.

In the course of time people became more and more con[-]

vinced that to be a good chess master without a satisfactory defensive technique was unthinkable, and in our own days we consider a good defence to be just as important as a faultless attacking plan, if not more so. The art of defence has been developed in a brief space of time. Once upon a time one could serenely sacrifice a pawn or a piece, according to circumstances, in order to set into motion some wished-for attack. In our own days we have to exert great care in such enterprises. A sacrifice must now lead to a tangible success, since otherwise the careful defensive player will, as a general rule, emerge with the win.

The aim in this chapter is not to teach the difficult art of defence. I have set myself a much lighter task, and in the ensuing pages I consider some cases where one side has to defend a difficult, or even possibly a lost, position. Unfortunately, it often happens, as is well known, that one meets with such situations and perhaps therefore some counsel drawn from my own experiences would not be without profit for the reader.

The latter might now ask: Why concern oneself with positions that are already lost? Provided the opponent plays the continuation correctly there is nothing in fact to be done, so why worry oneself to no purpose? No, let's just try a swindle and if that misfires then give up the game! However, it is not so simple as all that and it is against just such a conception that I direct myself in the following pages of this chapter. Lasker has already said that a position can never be so bad as not to offer prospects of defence, and therein lies a great truth. However hopeless the situation appears to be there yet always exists the possibility of putting up a stubborn resistance. And it is the player's task to find these opportunities and make the best of them. When the player with the upper hand is continually confronted by new problems, when, at every moment, one renders the win as difficult as possible, then it is likely that his powers will eventually weaken and he may make some mistake.

I think I will begin my examples with an old game. It was played in the first round of the grandmaster tournament at St Petersburg, 1914, and after Black's twenty-fourth move the following position occurred.

Bernstein

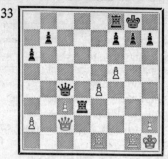

33

Janowski

It is not necessary to study the position over deeply to realize that Black has a clear advantage. Black's pieces are more actively placed; he enjoys possession of the only open file; on QR2, QB3, and K4 White has weak pawns that are difficult to defend – and so on. An attempt to hold the position by *25. R – Kt3* helps White not at all on account of *25. .... KR –Q1*, and it stands out quite clearly that White must soon lose material. So it is a bad outlook for White and from the purely objective standpoint he is probably lost. In what way can White still seek to save himself? In answering this question we shall first see what happened in the game. Janowski was, as is well known, a master who always strove after the attack and often distinguished himself by his tactical skill in this department of the game. Defence, as in the example quoted, did not suit him at all well, and so it is not surprising that White is in practice lost after a few moves.

25. P – K5?	Q – B3 ch
26. R – Kt2?	KR – Q1
27. Q – B2	R – Q7
28. Q – Kt3	R × R
29. Q × R	Q × P

With this the situation is clear. Janowski still tried *30. Q – Kt3, R – Q6; 31. Q – R4, R – R5; 32. Q – Kt3, Q – B3*

ch; *33.* K – Kt1, P – KR4; *34.* P – KR3, R – K5; *35.* P – K6,
but had to resign after the moves *35.* ..... P × P; *36.* P × P,
Q × P; *37.* R – KB1, R – K6; *38.* R – B3, R – K8 ch; *39.*
K – Kt2, Q × QRP ch.

So this has gone 'according to plan'. For us, however, the
interesting question is whether Black's position really was so
overwhelming as to yield a win without any difficulty. Here we
come for the first time into contact with the whole aim of this
chapter. We do not seek to claim in the ensuing paragraphs that
White's position was not lost, or that it could have been saved
by better play at some point or other. We shall only search for
some way in which White could have posed a greater problem
to his opponent and in this way created the possibility that his
adversary might not always find the right move. One should
never forget that chess is a game between two personalities and
not just a dry analysis of different possibilities.

Wherein then do White's chances lie? In the first place, he
must naturally try to coin an advantage from his two centre
pawns. If the pawns already were to stand on K5 and B5 then
he could create a dangerous passed pawn on the K file and thus
an eventual counter-attack on this point would gain in force.
In the second place, White should exploit the possibility of
counter-play along the KKt file. By means of these two possibilities Black could be hindered from trying to win in the attack,
and one might also hazard the assumption that there would
soon be an exchange of Queens. And White's main task resides
exactly in bringing about this Queen exchange in as favourable
a manner as possible.

To obtain counter-chances in the Rook end game that arises
after a Queen exchange White must try to create weaknesses in
the opponent's pawn position. For this purpose he must aim at
exchanging Queens himself on QB6 and thereafter utilizing the
pawns on QR6 and QB6 for a counter-attack. In that case Black
would already have considerable technical difficulties to sur-
mount before he could evaluate his small material advantage. If
all this, generally considered, should succeed is another question which is not really relevant.

In order to attain his goal White must proceed systematically

and therefore 25. P – K5 was already a step from the right
path. After 25. .... Q – B3 ch; 26. R – Kt2 leads, as we
already have seen, to a completely hopeless ending, and White
could have instead tried 26. Q – Kt2. However, Black would
have replied to this 26. .... R × P, retaining his pawns intact
on the Queen's wing, since the attempt to attack by 27. R – K4,
P – KKt3; 28. P – K6 is scarcely to be feared on account of
28. .... R – B7. So White must, in spite of everything, exchange down to a Rook end game, but under less favourable circumstances than he could have obtained with the best
play.

Once we have studied what has been said above then we can
soon find White's best chance. This lies in 25. Q – KKt2! which
threatens mate on KKt7 and affords Black no great choice in
reply.

25. Q – KKt2!	Q × BP

Black could also have tried 25. .... P – KKt3, which
perhaps, objectively considered, is best. White would likewise
then continue 26. P – K5, after which an immediate 27.
P – K6 would set up the eventual threat of Q × P. In that
case, too, Black would have difficult positional problems to
solve.

26. P – K5	Q – B3

After 26. ... P – KKt3; 27. P – K6, White would obtain a
dangerous counter-attack. After the text-move, Tarrasch in the
tournament book regards Black's position as won since the
attempt to attack by 27. R – K4, P – KKt3; 28. P – K6, is
repulsed by 28. .... R – Q7!

We have, however, laid out the whole play on other lines. We
are not endeavouring to bring about a dubious attack but we
aim at a Rook ending in which the opponent will be faced with
difficult technical problems.

27. Q × Q!	P × Q

Bernstein

34

Janowski
(Variation)

With this diagram position our interest in the game stops. We have shown that White, despite appearing to have a thoroughly lost position, could have posed his opponent difficult problems through a logically directed defence. It is clear that now White has excellent counter-chances. He could, for example, try *28.* R – Kt3, so as to exchange a pair of Rooks and in this manner shield his comparatively open King's position. But also *28.* P – B6, P – Kt3; *29.* P – K6, P × P; (*30.* P – K7! was threatened) *30.* R × P, leads to a position in which it is very difficult to demonstrate a win for Black. Thus, had White utilized all his defensive possibilities then the result of the game would not have been at all so clear, and at all events would have cost Black in addition a whole deal of trouble.

The example shown above is one of the common cases in which one has to defend oneself in the worse position but yet can reckon on a certain amount of counter-play. It is much worse to defend a position which in itself offers no prospect of active counter-play and in which one can only wait to see if the opponent can succeed in strengthening his position or not. Such positions are particularly difficult to hold and only a few masters are able to put up a successful resistance in them. Among these masters the ex-world champion Lasker was pre-eminent. We could quote many examples of cases in which

Lasker saved himself in situations where many another player would have long since thrown up the sponge. The following diagram provides a very impressive case.

Nimzovich

35

Lasker

This position occurred after the twenty-sixth move in the game Lasker–Nimzovich from the grandmaster tournament at St Petersburg, 1914. Lasker had played the middle game indifferently and eventually lost a pawn without obtaining anything approaching adequate compensation. Black has a clear advantage in the diagram position. He has not only a sound pawn more but also a beautifully posted Knight in the centre, whilst his pawn position reveals no weaknesses. Objectively considered, White's game is quite worthless and few players would be disposed to continue the struggle.

I think that most players would have tried a freeing action by exchanging off the strong Knight on K5 and continuing with 27. Kt – Kt5. Objectively considered, this is perhaps strongest and then White would, after 27. .... Kt × Kt; 28. B × Kt, be in a position to threaten the rather disagreeable 29. B – B6. However, with this continuation the position would be simplified, and the less material that remains the easier it is to utilize the material advantage. But if indeed the opponent is to be confronted by problems in realizing his material superiority then one must try to make these problems as difficult as possible.

With this in mind, Lasker courageously refrained from the thrust *27.* Kt – Kt5, Kt × Kt; *28.* B × Kt. A study of the position arising after these moves quickly convinces one that further simplifications will be forced after *28.* .... P – B5. White can scarcely allow the pin by *29.* R – B2, R – Kt1, and so *29.* Q – K4 is practically forced. Then, however, follows *29.* .... P – B6; *30.* R – KB2, R – Kt1! and now Black obtains a favourable pawn exchange equally after *31.* Q × KBP, Q × Q; *32.* R × Q, B × P, as well as after *31.* R × P, Q × P. The position has become simplified still more and in consequence the problem of exploiting his material advantage is easier for Black.

Lasker had quite another conception of the problem posed by the position. Despite the good play his adversary has for his pieces he threatens nothing concrete for the moment. The enemy pawns are blockaded, the weak KRP is sufficiently protected, and the Rooks stand ready to inaugurate eventual counter-play along the KKt file. In order to get any further Black must carry out a regrouping, and to arrive at a promising plan for this is not easy. Lasker therefore decided that his immediate task was to await events so as to see how his opponent's plans would develop. But this idea of waiting is tied up with the notion of seizing the opportunity during a regrouping on the opponent's part of organizing an eventual and successful counter-attack, thereby extracting himself from the difficult straits in which he lies. White's pieces cannot be better placed and so this leaves only a thoroughly passive waiting policy.

27.	P – R3	P – R3
28.	B – K3	R(R1) – Q1
29.	K – R2	R – R1
30.	K – R1	R(R1) – Q1
31.	K – R2	R – K1

As can be seen from these moves, Lasker has proved to be right with his waiting tactics. Nimzovich moves to and fro with his Rook and for the moment does not know how to proceed. It is naturally also possible that this last repetition of moves was dictated by time trouble.

As far as our investigations are concerned it does not matter

how Black ought to play so as best to utilize his advantage. The
plan to play both Rooks to the first rank, for example, deserves
consideration. The idea would be to follow it up thereafter by
Q – R1 and so take up the fight for control of the KKt file.
Nimzovich, however, chooses another plan. He wants, if possible, to continue with P – B3 and P – K4, and then make use of
his united passed pawns. So Lasker cannot remain passive any
longer and he therefore decides to exchange a pair of Rooks in
order subsequently to keep his opponent preoccupied by a
weakness on KB2.

In addition, here one might point out White's opportunity on
his thirty-first move of playing Kt – Kt5. After *31. . . . .*
Kt × Kt; *32.* B × Kt, White's Bishop would gain the square B6
and occupy an outpost there from which it could noticeably
impede Black's plans. Black, however, plays better *31. . . . .*
Q – R5; and after *32.* Kt × Kt (*32.* Kt – B3, Q – R4) *32. . . . .*
Q × Kt, his Queen gets into effective play. Lasker's waiting
method proves stronger.

Nimzovich

36

Lasker

32.	R–Kt8	R × R
33.	R × R ch	R – Q1
34.	R – Kt7	R – Q2
35.	R – Kt8 ch	R – Q1
36.	R – Kt7	R – B1

It should be observed that Nimzovich still does not know what procedure to adopt so as to increase his advantage. An exchange of the last pair of Rooks would undoubtedly make his task easier and therefore Lasker avoids it. The Rook's active position on Kt7 forces Black in turn to take up a defensive position for the time being, but it is clear that this state of things is purely temporary. In fact, the Rook can hardly be kept permanently stationed on Kt7, and, once it is driven away, Black can again turn his attention to the problem of how to get any further.

But what can Lasker do to exploit the temporarily active position of his pieces? With his next move he comes to the decision to harass his opponent by the eventual thrust of P – Q5 and in this manner to divert his attention from the strategic plan of Q – R1 followed by R – Kt1. So he must be prepared to go through the hurly-burly of a hand-to-hand fight without flinching.

37. P – B4   Kt – B3?

Lasker's tough and dour defence has perplexed Nimzovich and obviously caused him to lose the thread of the game. Strictly speaking, he still stands to win, and could indeed have most simply demonstrated this by logically following his strategic plan. Probably all Lasker's powerful defensive skill would not have availed him if Black had now played 37. .... Q – R1. If then 38. Q – Kt2, Black could continue successfully with 38. .... B – Q1, or 38. .... Kt – B3; and after 38. R – Kt2, Black could either have carried out his plan as in the game with 38. .... Kt – B3 or else taken up the fight along the important KKt file by 38. .... R – Kt1. It is hardly to be doubted that Black, by using such a systematic method of play, would eventually have won the game.

This consideration does not in the slightest diminish the importance of White's defensive strategy. It is impossible to hold good a lost position however skilfully one may be able to defend oneself. But one can again and again set the opponent difficult problems and this Lasker really has done with great skill. In actual practice it often occurs that the player with the

THE ART OF THE MIDDLE GAME

advantage plunges for inadequate methods if the solution to the problem is made sufficiently difficult for him the whole time. In such positions the motto is : fight to the end with all one's might and main !

> *38.* B – Kt5 !

Just one heedless move by the opponent and at once Lasker strikes ! Suddenly Nimzovich sees difficulties looming up (it is only too well known that such difficulties have a most depressing effect when they suddenly appear in a superior position. It is then that there come the horrid mistakes and oversights).

Probably Nimzovich thought at first that the worthy doctor had overlooked something with the Bishop move. Black can in fact continue with *38.* .... Kt – R4, and if the Rook occupies the only square *39.* R – R7, then there ensues *39.* .... Kt – B5 ! with a forced Queen exchange and an easily won ending for Black. Also pleasant for Black would be the possible simplification *39.* B – K7, Kt × R ; *40.* B × R, Kt – R4. And so perhaps without thinking any longer Nimzovich plumped for

> *38.* ....   Kt – R4 ?

This is what the wily old fox was waiting for ! But this move is the decisive mistake through which Black misses the fruits of his good play up to this point. Nimzovich was apparently disconcerted by the fact that after the Knight move *39.* B – K7 was threatened, followed by *40.* R × P. That *38.* .... Kt – K1 will not work on account of *39.* R × P, R × R ; *40.* Q × P ch, R – Q2 ; *41.* Kt – K5, can at once be comprehended. However, after *38.* .... Kt – Q2 White could have carried out his threat of *39.* B – K7, followed by R × P without risk. Guarding the Knight by *38.* .... B – Q1 also has its dark side. In the first place White can once again attack the point KB7 by *39.* Kt – K5, and in the second there also comes into consideration the idea *39.* B – B4, with the aim of exploiting the weakness on the diagonal KR2 – QKt8. So, suddenly, weaknesses appear in the façade of the good position and in such cases one seldom finds the best defence.

Had Nimzovich arrived at this situation from an equal position then he would have probably judged the chances for both sides more cold-bloodedly and would have then come to the conclusion that only by taking back his last move with *38. . . . . Kt – K5!* could there be prospects of retaining an advantage. Should White go in for winning a pawn by *39. B – K7, R – K1; 40. R × P,* then his pieces would be most precariously posted and he could scarcely hope to escape positional disadvantage. But that Black's task, even in this case, is nevertheless not so simple is shown by the following considerations.

One must first observe that direct attempts to utilize the hanging position of the Rook and Bishop on KB7 and K7 respectively lead to nothing. Thus, for example, Black gets nowhere after *40. . . . . Q – R4; 41. R – Kt7, Q – R3, 42. Q – Kt2, B – Kt6?* on account of *43. R × B, Kt × R; 44. B – Kt5!* etc. If, moreover, Black tries *41. . . . . Q – R1; 42. Q – Kt2, B – Kt6,* then White has the saving resource of *43. B – B6.*

Very strong for Black, however, is the quiet move *40. . . . . Q – Kt5!* which threatens *41. . . . . Q – Kt8.* If White plays in reply *41. R – B8, R × R; 42. B × R,* then he can resign after *42. . . . . Kt – Kt4!* Similarly, *41. B – Kt4,* also leads to loss of material on account of *41. . . . . P – R4* or *41. P – B4.* It seems as though White has nothing better than to return with his Bishop by *41. B – R4,* and with this we have arrived at the critical position.

Now *41. . . . . R – R1* looks very strong, but this would enable White to slip through Black's grasp by *42. B – B6!* If Black tries *41. . . . . Q – R4,* then there would follow *42. R – Kt7,* and after *41. . . . . Q – Kt3; 42. R – K7, R × R; 43. B × R,* White has got over the worst. After *41. . . . . Kt – Q3;* White also plays *42. R – K7,* and after *41. . . . . B – B5,* threatening *42. . . . . Kt – Q7,* White can defend his position by *42. Q – Q3.*

Black has however one continuation that takes advantage of his opponent's weaknesses, namely, *41. . . . . Q – Kt3; 42. R – K7, R – R1!* White's pieces are now very unfavourably placed and it is very dubious whether the threat of *43. . . . B – Q3* or *43. . . . . B – Q1* can be adequately parried. Equally, it should be observed that *41. .... R – R1; 42.* B – B6, R – Kt1, with the threat of *43. ....* Q – Kt3, also held out good prospects of success.

After the faulty sally with the Knight Lasker's great chance comes at last. He can reap the fruits of his good defence and execute a beautiful combination, long since planned, which secures him equality.

Nimzovich

37

Lasker

39. R × P!

This sacrifice which, moreover, is absolutely correct, must have come as a complete surprise to Nimzovich. It must have seemed that now in fact he even stood in danger of losing.

| *39. ....* | R × R |
| *40.* Q × P ch | R – Q2 |

Nor would *40. ....* K – Kt1 lead to any better result. It is true that then *41.* Q × R, would not do, but *41.* Q – K8 ch! puts everything right once again. After *41. ....* K – R2; *42.* Q × R, the Bishop on QB2 would be hanging and after *41. ....* B – Q1; *42.* B × B, not only is the Rook in danger but in addition mate is threatened by *43.* B – Kt6.

| *41.* Kt – K5 | B × Kt |
| *42.* Q – K8 ch | |

Here the players agreed a draw since after *42. . . . K – B2;43.*
Q × B ch, Black's King cannot escape perpetual check. A
wonderful defensive achievement by Lasker. One could quote a
host of examples like this in which Lasker rescued himself
from desperate situations through a resourceful defence. It was
said of him at the time that he made passes in order to exert a
psychological effect on his adversary. But, as we have seen,
neither passes nor hypnotism played the slightest role in such
cases. Lasker was purely and simply a great fighter who could
also put up a tough fight in inferior positions, in this way being
able to save many a difficult position.

There have, of course, existed many great masters of the
difficult art of defence in times past, and it is not possible for us
to tell of them all here, or to furnish proof of their defensive
achievements. Nor is that the aim of this chapter. But, when one
refers to defence in the game of chess, then one must not forget
one name, and that is, Capablanca. Many chess-players are
probably conscious above all that Capablanca's strength lay in
his well-known clarity of play, in a perfect technique, and in the
most impeccable intuition. But Capablanca's strength as a
defensive player has not been appreciated to the full. While
Lasker for the most part distinguished himself by his defence in
confused positions where his opponent had a certain advantage,
Capablanca's strength lay in quite another direction. In clear
positions, where he had the disadvantage, particularly in the
end game, Capablanca defended himself with remarkable cool-
ness and astonishing powers of resource, and we could show a
host of examples in which he saved apparently hopeless end
games. There existed very few masters indeed skilful enough to
utilize a small end-game advantage against Capablanca, who
understood as no other person how to avail himself of the
smallest possible chance.

To demonstrate one out of many examples let us examine the
position in the following diagram which is from a game Rubinstein–Capablanca, St Petersburg, 1914. This position occurred
after White's twenty-seventh move.

Capablanca

38

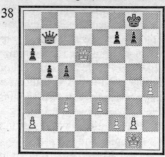

Rubinstein

White has a fine position in this Queen ending and at first glance one can hardly believe that Black will be able to avert loss. White has in the first place a sound pawn more, but this fact is not decisive by itself. As is well known, in Queen endings the most vital thing is not to have a pawn more but to have a passed pawn, this being of much greater importance. A strong passed pawn in a Queen ending is usually enough to compensate for a material disadvantage. However, in the diagram position Black, on the contrary, has no such advantage.

In the second place it should be observed that White's Queen is much more actively posted than Black's, and it not only threatens the pawn on QB5 but it also controls the more important central squares. Finally, in the third place, White's King is much more securely situated than Black's, this being no small advantage. So it can be seen that Capablanca's plight is not at all enviable.

How then, despite all this, can any counter-play with some hopes of success be organized? The pawn thrust 27. .... P – B5 obviously serves to threaten to create an eventual passed pawn by P – Kt5. Nevertheless, this move cannot be good, since White can utilize the time given him to play 28. P – B3 and thus deprive the enemy Queen of its last square in the centre. After that, 28. .... P – QR4 fails against 29. Q – Q8 ch, and the end game after 28. .... P – Kt5; 29. P × P, Q – B1; 30. Q – Q2,

P – B6; *31.* Q – QB2, Q – QB5; *32.* P – R3, would give White good prospects of making his material advantage tell by advancing the pawns on the King's wing. If Black remains passive after *28.* P – B3, then White plays *29.* P – R3 and has clearly the superior game.

The attempt to protect the pawn on QB4 by *27.* .... Q – B1 would also be insufficient. In reply White could secure his Queen's wing by P – QR3 and thereafter take measures to exploit his superiority on the opposing wing. In general, Black must not behave too passively and thus give White the occasion to advance his King-side pawns without having to worry about counter-play on the Queen's side. In that event White's win would be merely a question of time. Black must therefore find an active plan and hence Capablanca played with absolute correctness

27. ....   P – Kt5 !

He tries to create a passed pawn on the Queen's side at once, and, with this in view, he does not shun an eventual further pawn sacrifice. In the variation *28.* P × P, Q × P! *29.* Q × RP, P – B5; the QB pawn becomes so strong that White can scarcely hope to attain more than a draw. White has not much choice since in fact *28.* .... P × P is threatened.

28. Q × BP?

This capture confronts Black with the least difficulties and through this continuation we miss most of the finesses that lie concealed in Capablanca's plan. The main line of counter-play, and the one with which Capablanca obviously reckoned in the first place, was *28.* P – QB4!

After this pawn move Black, seemingly, gets into great difficulties, since how can he now guard his QB pawn? Immediately *28.* .... P – QR4 of course fails on account of *29.* Q – Q8 ch, nor does the immediate advance *28.* .... P – Kt6 prove adequate after *29.* P × P, Q × P; *30.* Q × RP. Nor does it seem at all attractive to protect the QBP with the Queen, since after *28.* .... Q – R2; *29.* Q – Q8 ch, K – R2; *30.* Q – R5, or also after 28. . . . . Q – B1; 29. Q – QKt6, both Queens would be temporarily out of play and White would be threatening a decisive strengthening of his position by an action on the King's side.

What then has Capablanca achieved by the thrust 27. . . . . P – Kt5? Was perhaps this move really not so strong and does it merely lead to fresh difficulties? And finally, why did such a subtle end-game artist refrain from the obvious move 28. P – QB4?

These questions are not so easily answered if one is not able to understand Capablanca's deeply conceived plan of defence. First it must be realized that Capablanca was playing to activate his Queen, and that with this aim he was prepared to sacrifice yet another pawn. By striking at the weaknesses in White's pawn position, a position which cannot be easily protected by the Queen, Capablanca seeks to inaugurate an effective counter-play. This could, it is true, have eventually led to a position in which White would have the material superiority of two pawns, but the realization of this advantage would have been associated with the greatest difficulties.

Now we must consider in what way Black can best sacrifice the second pawn. First 28. . . . . Q – K5 comes into consideration. If then 29. Q × RP, Black cannot at once play 29. . . . . Q – Kt8 ch; 30. K – R2, Q – B7; on account of 31. Q – B8 ch, followed by 32. Q × P. But, suddenly, after the quiet move 29. . . . . K – R2! Black would have an excellent position. The pawn on KR4 is attacked, White's Queen is tied down to the defence of QB4 and QR2, while after 30. P – Kt3, Q – Kt8 ch; 31. K – R2, Q – B7! White's King is in great trouble. Despite his extra two pawns White can scarcely hope to win this position.

The possibilities of the position are not completely exhausted with this, since after 28. . . . . Q – K5, White is not indeed forced to capture at once on QR6, but can concern himself with the pawn on QB5. After 29. Q × BP, Q – Kt8 ch; 30. K – R2, Q × P; 31. Q × P, Q × KBP the end game seems at first glance to be very comfortable for Black. He has in fact only one pawn less, possesses a passed pawn on the QR file, and in addition the

White King is exposed to attack. Despite all this, the position is not satisfactory for Black, chiefly on the grounds of White's dangerous passed pawn on the QB file. White continues with *32. Q – K7!* and it is not easy to see how the victorious career of the QBP is to be stopped. Thus the counter-attack by *28. .... Q – K5* is not adequate and we must therefore look further.

The next idea that comes into consideration is the Queen manoeuvre *28. .... Q – R2; 29. Q – Q8 ch, K – R2; 30. Q – R5, Q – K2!* After *31. Q × RP,* Black can either win back a pawn by *31. .... Q × RP,* or else transpose into a position we have already considered by *31. .... Q – K5.* In these variations everything is perfectly in order for Black. The situation becomes more complicated, however, when White refrains from moving the Queen to QR5 and utilizes the Black Queen's passive position on QR2 to embark on some quick action on the King's side. After *29. P – Kt4, P – R4; 30. P – R5, P – R5; 31. P – Kt5,* we arrive at a position in which the issue hangs on a hair. It seems however that White's attack can be successfully met by e.g. *31. .... P – Kt6; 32. P – Kt6, Q – R1; 33. P × P, P – R6;* and now Black can coolly defend himself after either *34. Q – Q7,* or *34. Q – K7,* by *34. .... P – R7!* The situation is complicated and a clear winning method for White is not to be found; so *28. .... Q – R2* would seem to ensure Black a satisfactory defence.

Let us also examine the possibility of *28. .... Q – B1* which prevents an advance on the King's side and, practically speaking, forces *29. Q – QKt6* on account of the threat of *29. .... P – R4.* Now Black has not the time to prepare his ensuing manoeuvre by *29. .... K – R2,* since then White would gain possession of the vital KB5 square by *30. P – K4,* and so obtain excellent winning chances. Black is forced to offer up another pawn by *29. .... Q – B4!* which White would swallow up by *30. Q × RP.* Now there comes *30. .... K – R2!* and we have the position in which, as already mentioned, the realization of the two-pawn advantage is associated with great difficulties.

Capablanca

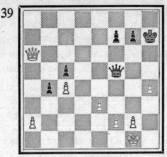

Rubinstein
(Variation)

Should White, for example, play *31*. Q – R4, then there
could follow *31*. .... Q – Kt8 ch; *32*. K – R2, Q – B4 and the
protection of the pawn on KB2 would cost White a great deal of
trouble. In addition, *32*. .... Q – Kt7 would appear to be
worthy of consideration here. After *31*. Q – R5, Black has the
strong reply *31*. .... Q – K4! at his disposal, after which he
threatens *32*. .... Q – R8 ch, followed by *33*. .... P – Kt6.
After *32*. Q – R4, Q – R8 ch a position arises similar to that we
have mentioned above.

The most dangerous move for Black is however *31*. Q – R7,
which attacks both the pawns on QB5 and KB7, but even on
this move Black should obtain counter-play. In the first place he
can quietly play *31*. .... P – B3, and prepare the threat of
32. .... Q – K4, and in the second place *31*. .... Q – K4 at
once also merits consideration. After *32*. Q × KBP, Q – R8
ch; *33*. K – R2, Q × P, the QKt pawn is a factor to be reckoned
with, and it is obvious that White can get nowhere with his
attack against the King.

From the variations given above we can see that Black, after
28. P – QB4 (White's best continuation) had two lines sufficient
to yield him good prospects of a draw. With this we have shown
how deeply thought out Capablanca's defensive idea of P – Kt5!
really was. This was the reason in fact why Rubinstein did not
allow himself to try the continuation *28*. P – QB4, leaving the

chess world without a chance of witnessing the beautiful main
idea of the variation.

28.	P × P
29. Q × P	Q – Kt8 ch
30. K – R2	Q × P

Now Black's task is much simpler, since in his passed pawn
on the QR file he has a powerful factor that nullifies every
attempt to win on the part of his adversary. At the moment the
pawn on KB2 is attacked and must be protected.

31. Q – B8 ch	K – R2
32. Q – B5 ch	P – Kt3
33. Q – B6	P – R4

By reason of his passed pawn Black's position is so strong that
he might have, had he so desired, tried for a win by 33. ....
Q – K3! Since, however, he is content with a draw, the continuation in the text is the simplest.

34. P – Kt4	P – R5
35. P – R5	P × P

Now, playing for a win does not come into question since
35. .... Q – K3? fails against 36. P × P ch, and if he falls for
the bait of 35. .... P – R6 then 36. P – R6! K × P?; (36. ....
Q – Kt7 was essential) 37. Q – R8 ch, K – Kt 4; 38. K – Kt3,
leads to a forced mate on R4.

36. Q – B5 ch

Rubinstein rightly refrains from further attempts to win and
forces the draw as quickly as possible, since he could even have
lost the game after, for example, 36. P × P, Q – K3!

36.	K – Kt2
37. Q – Kt5 ch	K – R2
38. Q × P ch	K – Kt2

Drawn.

It is indeed wonderful to observe the ease with which Capablanca has conducted this difficult ending to a drawn position.

We have now, by some examples, demonstrated the great skill in defence of difficult positions forthcoming from the whilom world champions, Lasker and Capablanca, on the occasions when they were hard pressed. We could of course add to this list of efforts of great defensive artistry, but, within the limits of this chapter, we must content ourselves with these two master-pieces.

In the ensuing pages I should like to elucidate some positions from modern tournament practice in which one side is saddled with a difficult defence, and, to some extent at any rate, is able to solve the problem successfully. To begin with, here is an interesting position from the game Samisch–Prins, Hastings Christmas Congress, 1938–9.

Prins

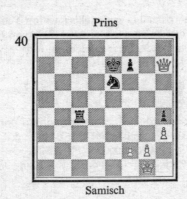

40

Samisch

Materially White has the advantage and should normally win without much difficulty. But matters are not so simple since the remaining material is confined to one wing only, a factor which favours the defence. On the other hand, it seems scarcely credible that Black can, nevertheless, still mobilize something resembling a valid defence. And White would indeed have won the game without trouble had he not underestimated the defensive resources of his opponent.

It should at once be observed that White must create for himself a passed pawn in order to force the win. And this can be easily brought about if he plays P – Kt4 and then advances the passed R pawn. In principle then the winning method is very simple and it is almost incredible that this method can come up against any practical difficulties. So now there came

1. P – Kt4

Black's situation is now difficult, if not to say hopeless. He has to exchange on Kt6 in order not to lose the pawn on R5, and then the KR pawn becomes a powerful factor in the game. A struggle against this pawn and the Queen with the Rook and Knight must be hopeless in the long run – as doubtless Prins, too, said to himself. But what is to be done otherwise?

In this desperate plight the Dutch master hit upon an extraordinary idea. How would it be if he gave up the Knight for the R pawn and then sought salvation in an ending with Rook against Queen? It is well known that in such cases where Black has a pawn on KB2 and his opponent is left with only a KKt pawn the position is drawn. With this in mind he took appropriate action.

Had Samisch also thought of this idea he would certainly not have been in such a hurry to make the thrust *1.* P – Kt4. First of all *1.* Q – R8 and then P – Kt4 would have most simply solved the problem of the position and quickly resulted in a won game. But we shall see what actually happened.

| 1. .... | P × P e.p. |
| 2. P × P | Kt – Kt4 |

Black must not delay carrying out his plan since once White contrives to get in *3.* P – R4, the win is easy.

| 3. Q – B5 | Kt × P ch! |
| 4. Q × Kt | R – B3 |

Black has put up the best possible defence and attained a position that still sets White many problems. Even if the position, despite everything, should still be lost nevertheless Prins, at all events, has set his opponent new and difficult tasks and has therefore acquired fresh hope for himself. Samisch was manifestly completely taken aback and hence played in a way that allowed Prins to arrive at a position with White K on B5, Q on QB3, P on KKt4, Black K on Kt1, R on K3, and P on KB2. Such a position is in fact drawn and the players contented themselves with a friendly division of points. So Prins's happy idea of defence proved successful and salvaged half a point from a practically hopeless loss.

Had not White lost his self-command when faced by his opponent's surprising defence then he would scarcely have failed to see that there was in reality one and one only very difficult winning line and indeed no certain draw. White committed his decisive mistake when he allowed Black's King to attain the KKt1 square. Had White pinned down the King to the K file then in so doing he would have assured himself a won game. Since the end game is extremely interesting we shall, in the ensuing lines, examine more closely how matters should have been conducted to force the win. The following moves are naturally not forced, but the position that arises after the twelfth move could have been obtained by White against any defence.

5.	Q – R4 ch	K – K1

After 5. .... P – B3 White's task would be easier since then he would also have the chance of attacking the King from the seventh rank. Black can put up the stiffest resistance by retaining his pawn on B2 to the end.

6.	Q – R8 ch	K – K2
7.	K – B2	R – KKt3

There is nothing else for Black to do but to remain on the qui vive and make waiting moves. However he plays, he cannot prevent White from obtaining the position in the following diagram.

8.	K – B3	R – K3
9.	K – Kt4	R – Kt3 ch
10.	K – R5	R – K3

Naturally 10. R × P, will not do on account of 11. Q – K5 ch.

| 11. P – Kt4 | R – KKt3 |
| 12. P – Kt5 | R – K3 |

Prins

41

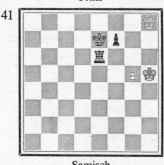

Samisch
(Variation)

This is the critical position which White can always force and in which a win can be shown by analysis. The following winning line is easy to understand.

| 13. Q – QKt8! | R – KKt3 |

The only move. After *13. . . . . R – Q3; 14. Q – B7 ch*, White succeeds eventually in exchanging off the last pawn by **P – Kt6**.

| 14. Q – Kt4 ch | K – K1 |

Again forced, since after other King moves there comes *15. . . . . Q – B8*, and *14. . . . . R – Q3* allows other winning continuations, e.g. *15. Q – Kt7 ch, K – K1; 16. Q – Kt8 ch, K – K2; 16. Q – B7 ch*, followed by an eventual **P – Kt6**, etc.

| 15. Q – K4 ch | R – K3 |

Or *15. . . . . K – B1; 16. Q × R!, P × Q ch; 17. K × P, K – Kt1; 18. K – R6*, winning easily.

16. Q × R ch!	P × Q
17. K – R6 and White wins since the Kt pawn marches	
on unhindered to Queen.	

As has been seen, the defence found by Prins did not ensure the draw, but it set his opponent fresh problems in an easily won position and this in turn led to Black being eventually able to salvage half a point.

A very fine example of cool defence is to be found in the game Smyslov–Polugayevsky from the U.S.S.R. Championship in Moscow, 1961. In this encounter the following position occurred after White's nineteenth move.

Polugayevsky

42

Smyslov

Polugayevsky had played the middle game indifferently and in the diagram position his game is far from enviable. White has succeeded in building up a powerful pawn centre, and both his Bishops are dangerously aimed at the Black monarch. If White manages to carry out the thrust then Black can quietly regard his position as ripe for resignation.

But what can Black do in his difficult situation? Against the threat of *20. P – Q5*, there is certainly a defence by *19. . . . . Kt – B3*, but what course should Black take, for example, after *20. R – B3*, or even *20. P – KKt4*? He would then be placed in a totally passive position without any counter-play, and sooner or later his game must collapse. At the first glance *19. . . . . P – B3* seems satisfactory, since after *20. Kt × Kt, Q × Kt*, White can no longer protect the QB4 square and hence Black has adequate compensation for the weakness on K3. But

19. .... P – B3 has a rather serious disadvantage, to wit, the tactical thrust *20. P(QB4) – B5!* After the ensuing forced continuation *20. .... B × B; 21. Kt × B, P × P; 22. Q × P ch,* Black must play *22. .... Kt – B2* if he wishes to avoid still worse. After *23. QR – K1!, P × P; 24. Kt – Q5* (also very strong is *24. Kt – Kt5, B – B4; 25. Kt × B, Kt × Kt; 26. Q × Q, KR × Q; 27. R × R ch, R × R; 28. B × P, P – QR3; 29. B × Kt, P × Kt; 30. R – Kt1) 24. .... B – Q3; 25. Q – Kt4, Q – Q1; 26. B × P,* his position, however, is completely undermined and it is very doubtful whether he can make any stand against the concentrated force of White's pieces. In any case, one never chooses such a variation of one's own free will.

After long cogitation Polugayevsky eventually found a solution that must be regarded as the only correct one from the practical point of view. He courageously decided to accept his adversary's pawn sacrifice and played

19.	Kt × Kt !
20. BP × Kt	Kt × P

The position still appears as quite the reverse of bright for Black since, though indeed he has solved his troubles and problems in the centre, his King has suddenly become exposed to all sorts of dangerous threats. One must possess both courage and a faculty for exact calculation to venture forth from such a position. Of course, Polugayevsky would hardly have done so had he any other possibility at his disposal, but from the diagram position onwards this sharp-edged continuation afforded the best possibilities. Only if Black is not mated can he then indeed have good prospects of survival.

21. Kt – K4	Q – Q1

Black must neither now nor in many variations later play *21. .... Kt × B,* since after *22. B × B,* at the least he would lose the exchange. However, *22. Kt – B6 ch!* is also threatened. The attack on White's centre inaugurated by the text-move is in fact directed against this threat and is without any doubt Black's best defensive chance.

22. Kt – B6 ch

Even now the sacrifice is very strong but it is far from being immediately decisive. Likewise it is difficult to see how White can strengthen his attack after *22.* Q – R5, P – R3, since *23.* Kt – B6 ch can be coolly answered by 23. .... K – R1. White has also to reckon with the counter-threat of *22.* .... Kt × B; *23.* B × B, Q × P ch.

It is naturally much easier to ascertain after subsequent home analysis what the best continuation seems to be. But the game itself is played in quite another atmosphere, and here one must choose the best chance among all the enticing variations that are to be found. In addition, it should be observed that these variations are for the most part extremely complicated, and if one makes a small oversight then the result may be complete and utter defeat. Every tournament player knows how difficult it is to find the right method of attack from among the many possibilities that offer themselves.

Afterwards, the Knight check was criticized (but wrongly, as we soon shall see) and instead the quiet preparatory move *22.* K – R1, was recommended. It is perhaps correct that this move would have given White better results. But, on the other hand, one should also realize that this quiet move would afford the opponent many defensive possibilities, and these must be accurately calculated by White. Apart from the fact that one has to refute Black's useful *22.* .... Q – Q4, one must in addition demonstrate that the continuation *22.* .... Kt × B; *23.* B × B, Q × P; *24.* B × R, R × B; *25.* Kt – Q6, B × Kt; *26.* P × B, P – Kt3 is untenable for Black. I cannot believe that the problem of the position would have been better solved by *22.* K – R1.

After the move played, hair-raising complications arise during which Black's fate hangs by a thin thread. This is a situation that is indeed not altogether agreeable for Black, but in view of his precarious plight it is only to be desired, since it is in fact in complicated positions that one most often notices cases where the adversary fails from time to time to make the best move.

22. ....   B × Kt

Naturally not *22. ....* P × Kt, whereupon *23.* Q – Kt4 ch,
K – R1; *24.* P × P, B × P; *25.* Q – K4, leads to a clear win.
Also *22. ....* K – R1; *23.* Kt × P!, Kt × B; *24.* B × B,
Q × P ch; *25.* K – R1, results in a position where Black must at
least lose the exchange (*25. ....* K × Kt; *26.* B × R, R × B;
27. Q – R5 ch, K – Kt1; *28.* Q × P ch, etc.). The text-move
allows the adversary the least freedom of choice and is therefore
the best.

23. P × B   Kt × B

It is a debatable question as to whether Black could have tried
to meet White's attack by *23. ....* P – Kt3, and in this way
attempted to render his advantage in material effective. Tactic-
ally, this continuation is irreproachable, since a direct mating
attack by *24.* B × Kt, B × B; *25.* Q – K3, B × R; *26.* R × B,
is repulsed by *26. ....* K – R1; *27.* Q – R6, R – KKt1;
28. R – B3, Q – B1. But White need not be in such a hurry. I
regard the strong outpost on KB6, the weakened King-side
position and the two Bishops as more than sufficient compensation for the pawn sacrifice. There are many continuations, e.g.
24. Q – KB2, Q – Q4; *25.* Q – B4, B – Kt2; *26.* R – B3, or
also quite simply *24.* R – B4, by which White could retain a
redoubtable initiative, and which should soon lead to a tangible
result.

It is naturally a question of taste which of these two continuations one would recommend for Black. In both cases White
preserves an incontestable advantage and this is in fact quite
natural when one takes into consideration the difficulties with
which Black has to contend in the diagram position.

24. B × P ch!

White must continue in sacrificial style since in the quiet
variation *24.* B × B, Q × P ch; *25.* R – B2, Black saves himself
by *25. ....* Kt – Q6! The sacrifice is nevertheless colossally
strong and it is undoubtedly a marvel that Black is not mated as
a result. One must admire Polugayevsky's intuition in being able

to foresee that he could emerge from all the ensuing complications with a more or less whole skin.

For the rest, the quiet continuation 24. Q – Kt4, P – Kt3; 25. B × B, also comes into question, since, in the strong pawn on KB6 and the bad position of the Black Knight White has certainly more than adequate compensation for his pawn. After 25. .... R – B7 there could follow 26. B – Kt7, and if then 26. .... R – Q7, then 27. P – Q5, with the threat of 28. Q – B4. But the sacrifice on R7 is much more forcing and should have given White a clear advantage.

24. ....   K – R1

Naturally, not 24. K × B; 25. Q – R5 ch, K – Kt1; 26. Q – Kt5, when Black has to give up his Queen. After the move played the game has reached its culminating point. Black has, it is true, a piece more, but his King is exposed to attack from many White pieces and one can scarcely believe that he will manage to emerge with a whole skin. We will, however, come to see that there still exist some unexpected and different defensive possibilities in Black's position, and these will render White's task more difficult.

Polugayevsky

Smyslov

25. Q – Kt4?

Smyslov weakens under the influence of his adversary's

resourceful and dour defence and hence he does not find the best line for the attack, but allows his opponent to emerge unscathed from the whole affair. As was shown earlier, it seems scarcely credible that Black should be able to defend himself in this position. Despite the continuous difficulties there must be an attacking continuation for White, unless his position should chance to be pursued by a perverse fate.

At the first glance the text-move also seems highly promising, since Black is now forced to capture on KB3, when his bare King should succumb to the attack along the KR file. As the continuation shows, however, this is not so, and therefore we must deem the text-move a mistake through which White misses a well deserved win. The question now is: how should White have continued so as to strengthen his attack in decisive fashion?

The answer to this question lies in the direct attacking move 25. Q – R5! which threatens mate in two moves and forces the reply 25. .... Q × P ch. Now 26. R – B2, seems at first sight very attractive since White, after 26. .... Q – K6, appears to win the exchange by 27. B – Q3 dis ch, Q – R3; 28. Q × Q ch, P × Q; 29. B × B. However, Black replies 26. .... B – K7! and repels the attack, since 27. Q – R3, can be simply met by 27. .... Q – KKt5. So White must continue with 26. K – R1.

Now mate is again threatened and the only defence consists in interposing the Queen on KR3. This must be done at once since the insertion of 26. .... B – K7, would result in catastrophic consequences. White in fact plays 27. R – B3! and after 27. .... B × R; 28. P × B, the open KKt file is decisive: 28. .... Q – K6; 29. B – K4 dis ch, Q – R3; 30. P × P ch, K × P; 31. R – Kt1 ch and wins, since 31. .... Q – Kt3; 32. R × Q ch, leads to an immediate mate. So there is nothing else for Black but 26. .... Q – K6.

In this position a direct mating attack cannot break through, and White must therefore attempt to regain his sacrificed material. He has only a piece less and this is easy to regain by 27. B – Q3 dis ch, Q – R3; 28. P × P ch, K × P; 29. Q – Kt4 ch, K – R1; 30. B × B. The storm has now died down and we can begin to set about surveying the result. What has in fact White achieved?

Just a fleeting glance at the position reveals to us that White has a considerable positional advantage. One might go even further and maintain that White has a won position. He has hardly begun to shed any material – only one little pawn – and in return for this he has several positional trump cards in his hand. Black's King-side position has been broken up, his Knight is completely misplaced, and in addition the Rook on QB1 is *en prise*. More one cannot ask for in return for a little pawn!

In order to convince even the greatest sceptics I will append some variations in proof of this. It is clear that Black must move the attacked Rook since no exchange sacrifice can come into question. Let us commence with *30. . . . . QR – Q1*. The most convincing variation would run as follows: *31. R – B3, P – B4*; (*31. . . . . R – KKt1*; *32. Q – Kt4*, leads to similar lines) *32. Q – Kt4, Q – B3*; *33. R – QKt1, R – Q8 ch* (after *33. . . . . P – Kt4*; *34. P – Kt4* is very strong, but even the simple *34. B × P* is good enough); *34. R × R, Kt × R*; *35. B – K2, R – Q1*; *36. R – R3 ch, K – Kt2*; *37. R – Kt3 ch, K – R1 (or R2)*; *38. Q – KB4*, and it is difficult to see what Black can do against the threat of *39. Q – B3*.

Now let us explore the next possibility, *30. . . . . R – B7*. White then continues with *31. R – B3*, which threatens *32. R – KR3*, and, practically speaking, forces the answer *31. . . . . P – B4* since *31. . . . . R – KKt1*; *32. Q – Q4 ch*, or *31. . . . . R – B8 ch*; *32. R × R, Q × R ch*; *33. B – B1*, both lead to an immediate loss for Black. Among the many possibilities that now present themselves to White, he can, successfully, choose the following line: *32. Q – Kt4!, Q – B3*; (after *32. . . . . K – Kt1*; *33. Q – Kt3, R – Q7*; *34. R – K1* is very strong, since among other things it threatens *33. R – KR3*) *33. Q – Kt3, R – Q7*; (or *33. . . . . R – B4*; *34. R – QKt1, P – Kt4*; *35. B × P*, and Black cannot play *35. . . . . R – QKt1* on account of *36. R – R3 ch*, followed by *37. Q – Kt3 ch*) *34. R – K1*, and Black's position is hopeless. After *34. . . . . R – K1*, White can, for instance, proceed with *35. R × BP!, Q × R*; *36. Q – B3* ch, K – Kt1; *37*. Q × R, even if he has not higher pretensions. In any case there can hardly exist any doubt as to the final result.

Finally, I might also mention the possibility of *30*. .... R – B4, with the crafty notion of meeting *31*. QR – Kt1, with *31*. .... R – KR4! If now *32*. R × Kt?, then Black wins the exchange by *32*. .... R × P ch; *33*. K – Kt1, R – R8 ch; *34*. K – B2, R × R ch followed by *35*. .... Q – B8 ch or *35*. .... Q – B3 ch; while if *32*. P – KR3, then *32*. .... R – R5 and the Knight escapes via QR5. But neither will this resource save Black. White's best play is *31*. Q – Kt4!, Q – Kt2; (or 31. .... R – B7; *32*. R – B3, etc.) *32*. R – B3, R – KKt4 (*32*. .... Kt – Q6 results in the loss of the Queen after *33*. Q – R4 ch, and on *32*. .... R – KR4 there can follow quite simply *33*. R – R – QKt1); *33*. R – QKt1!, R × P; *34*. R – R3 ch, K – Kt1; *35*. B – Kt7, and after winning the Knight White's remaining task is merely a question of technique.

Thus we have shown that Smyslov could have won with *25*. Q – R5! The win, however, was not easy to find, and, as we have seen, Black is very near saving himself in many variations, even with the best play. So Polugayevsky's courageous strategy has triumphed, and his resolute decision on the nineteenth move deserves the utmost recognition. With skilful play a difficult defensive position can be held even against a player of Smyslov's world champion class. The main thing is to keep on confronting the opponent with difficult problems, since solving these over the board is always most difficult.

25. ....   P × P

This is forced, as is easy to see, but it is also adequate. White no longer has at his command any continuation for strengthening the attack.

26. R – B4

Very strong seems first *26*. R – B3, with the intention of eventually setting up a mating threat by some Bishop move. Against this Black has only one defence, but that is also sufficient, namely *26*. .... R – B5! By means of the threat against

Q5 the enemy pressure is diverted and the possible Queen win
by 27. B – K4, Q × P ch; 28. K – R1, Q × B; 29. R – R3 ch,
Q – R2; 30. R × Q ch, K × R; 31. Q – R3 ch, K – Kt2; 32.
Q – Kt3 ch, K – R2 leads only to a draw. White must not indeed
embark on the win of a piece by 33. Q – R3, on account of
33. .... KR – B1; 34. Q × Kt, R – B7 (35. Q – R3, R(B1) –
B6!), and if anybody has winning chances then it is Black rather
than White.

After the text-move matters again look critical for Black,
since the Queen threatens to go to the KR file, with a menace of
mate. But this again can be met by an adequate defence.

26. ....   P – B4!

Naturally not 26. .... R – KKt1 because of 27. B × R,
Q × B; 28. Q – R3 ch, winning the Queen, or perhaps still
stronger, 27. Q – R3, R – Kt2; 28. R – R4, with the threat of
mate. The attempt, too, by 26. .... R – K1, to procure a flight
square via KB1 for the King, would have had a tragic end for
Black since White, in addition to 27. Q – Kt3, could also continue very strongly with 27. Q – R3, K – Kt2; 28. R – Kt4 ch,
K – B1; 29. Q – R3 ch!, in this way achieving a won position.
The text-move forces a clarification of the position.

27. B × P

White must concede the draw since after 27. Q – R5, K –
Kt2; or 27. Q – R3, Q – Kt4! Black would be able to make
determined efforts to win.

27. ....   P × B
28. R × P

White gets no further after 28. Q – R3 ch, K – Kt2; 29.
Q – Kt3 ch, K – B3.

28. ....   B – Q6!

Everything fits together almost as in an end-game study!
Now, after 29. R – R5 ch, the Bishop can intervene on R2.
The attack is at an end, and White must make the draw sure as
speedily as possible.

29. Q – R5 ch

Whereupon the players contented themselves with a draw,
White having a perpetual check with his Queen. A magnificent
struggle and at the same time a triumph for a courageous and
well thought-out plan of defence. The more one plays through
such games the more one tends to think that in our time it ought
to be an impossibility to break through a good defence.

Now, so as to illustrate how one defends difficult, well-nigh
hopeless, positions I will also give an example from my own
tournament play. In the game Bronstein–Keres at the Candidates' Tournament in Amsterdam, 1956, the following position
arose after White's thirty-sixth move.

Keres

44

Bronstein

Black's plight is wretched in the extreme. White has, it is
true, no plus in material, but his pieces command the whole
board and it seems to be merely a matter of time before Black's
position collapses. A cramped position is not in itself a disaster,
but if, in addition, one has no prospects of counter-play then
the situation usually becomes quickly hopeless. This, too, is the
case here. When one considers Black's plausible moves then it
soon becomes apparent that he can scarcely move anything
without incurring a speedy loss. The Queen and the Knight are
tied to the pawn on Q3; the Rook on R2 must protect the
Knight, and the Bishop on Q2 has only one move, to K1. One

E

can hardly think of a more hopeless situation, but even in such a position one ought to try to find some satisfactory method of defence.

Of course the reader will understand that I am not attempting to prove that Black's position is to be held by good defensive moves. That would be an insoluble problem, since White has a won game. Instead, the aim in this example is to demonstrate that even a position that is ripe for resignation can, despite everything, afford defensive possibilities that make the opponent's task more difficult. The game's final outcome depended less on my good defence, since in reality nothing like this is to be found, than on the psychological effect that my obstinate 'never surrender' tactics had on my opponent. These represent, however, the only kind of tactics that one can employ in such positions.

Now, however, back to the game. What can Black try in the diagram position? Naturally, nothing. But this does not mean that he should wander planlessly to and fro, waiting to see how White will consummate his advantage for a win. In every position, no matter how bad it may be, there always exist chances for small finesses, which one must employ whenever possible. It should never be forgotten that, in a superior position, one is always looking for a clear way to win. Quite often small advantages are despised, since one wants to obtain more out of the position. This factor, easily understood from the psychological angle, must be utilized, since thereby one can often embark on variations which one would never have been wont to try in equal positions. Psychological methods of warfare are the only possibilities in such positions.

In the diagram position White threatens to win a pawn by 36. Kt × QP, since after the capture the Rook on R7 is hanging. This threat is not to be parried by 35. . . . . . R(B1) – QR1. By this move Black would place his one more or less well-posted piece in a very passive position, and then he would have only his King and Bishop with which to play. Such passive positions rapidly collapse. Another question is whether White will most simply solve his problem by 36. P – B4, or in another way. Black must try for counter-play, however indifferent it may seem.

Hence therefore I hit upon the idea of allowing my opponent to carry out his threat at the cost of a pawn. And so I played

35. ....   B – K1!

This move is certainly the best under the given circumstances. If White carries out his threat by 36. Kt × QP, then Black replies 36. .... Kt × Kt; 37. R × Kt, Q × R; 38. Q × R, Q – Kt5! (to make this move possible, the Bishop must vacate the Q2 square) and suddenly obtains strong counter-play. After 39. Q × P, R – B8 ch; 40. K – R2, Q × KtP; 41. R – R2, Q – Kt6 Black can, as compensation for the pawn, create many threats that may cause his opponent anxiety. Such a result from the wretched position in the diagram would not be bad.

The text-move is also directed against other possibilities, such as, for instance, 36. P – B4. Upon this, Black now has the tactical possibility of 36. .... P × P; 37. Q × P, R × Kt!; 38. B × R, Q – B2, as a result of which he would once again emerge with an excellent game (39. R – Kt4, Kt – B4!). It is such small tactical finesses that constitute Black's chief weapon with the aid of which he will render his opponent's task more difficult. But against such a player as Bronstein success is not to be obtained by so simple a means.

36. P – QKt4!

Despite, or perhaps on account of, time trouble* Bronstein does not embark on the variations shown above, but instead continues to increase the pressure. Such tactics are naturally most unwelcome to the defence, the player of which must reckon for the whole time with specific threats. In addition, there has suddenly emerged a new problem child in the shape of the pawn on QR4. An extremely painful situation for Black, but one which, provisionally at any rate, he can just about protect.

36. ....   P – R5

The attempt to hold the pawn by 36. .... R(B1) – R1 would

* In competitive chess players are usually required each to make forty moves in two and a half hours and sixteen moves in every subsequent hour (Ed.)

not have helped since White would in any case have continued with *37.* P – Kt5. Either on QR4 or on QR5 the pawn would constitute a marked weakness.

Now there follow some neutral moves in time trouble, made so as to get clear of the time control. It is very awkward for Black that he is not able to force White to simplify, since it is much easier for White to work out a good plan of attack by analysis at home rather than in the fifth hour of play over the board. But now he can do nothing more to further this aim, as he has already devoted every opportunity to forcing the course of play along as much as possible.

37.	K – R2	R(R2) – R1
38.	B – K2	R – B2
39.	P – Kt5 !	

Preparing an exchange sacrifice on QB6, the effects of which Black is scarcely likely to survive. At the same time it practically circumscribes the effective power of the Black pieces altogether. Bronstein is conducting the game in really outstanding style.

The fact that the text-move gives up control of the QB5 square is of slight importance, since Black cannot occupy it with either Knight or Rook, on account of the reply *40.* Kt × QP. Now the pawn on QR5 is no longer protected by the Bishop, and it is clear that this pawn most fall, sooner or later. Black's only chance lies in seeking to obtain maximum compensation for this pawn by various tactical finesses.

39.	Q – Q1

Otherwise perhaps White would hit on the idea of initiating an aggressive plan of play on the other wing by *40.* P – B4, since the reply of *40.* .... R(R1) – B1 that was facilitated by the P – Kt5 move would now be quite without effect on account of *41.* R – B6. With the text-move this advance is prevented since after *40.* P – B4, P × P; *41.* Q × P, R × Kt; *42.* R × Kt, R – B2 Black would escape from his difficulties. The adversary must be kept continually busy with the aid of such small finesses !

40. R – R2   K – Kt2
41. R – B6

Bronstein's sealed move, and undoubtedly the best. *41.* P –
B4 would not be at all good here on account of *41.* ....
P × P; *42.* Q × P, R × Kt, and since the point KB7 is guarded
White must also reckon with the eventual continuation of
41. .... R × Kt; *42.* B × R, Kt – B4. As Bronstein intends
playing R – B6 sooner or later and this fits in with his plan of
play in the game it is best to make the move at once. In carrying
out this move, however, Bronstein was guilty of the unpardon-
able sin of using up thirty-five minutes of his precious time on
the clock. As we shall see later, this circumstance played a
decisive part in the further progress of the game.

Keres

45

Bronstein

It was in this difficult position that I commenced my analysis
of the adjourned game, a labour that obviously furnished me
with little pleasure. Firstly I convinced myself that acceptance
of the exchange sacrifice by *41.* .... B × R; *42.* QP × B, Kt –
B4; *43.* Kt × KP, was bad, because of the many threats, e.g.
44. Kt – Kt4, or *44.* P – Kt6, which would allow of no defence.
So Black must look further and await a favourable opportunity
of accepting the exchange sacrifice. Then there was not really
much to analyse and after some fruitless attempts I decided
upon a continuous waiting policy so as to see how my opponent

intended winning. However, so as to provide the utmost opposition to my adversary I decided to offer him the bait of the pawn on QR5.

41. ....   R – Kt1

This move was visibly a surprise to Bronstein and once again he thought for quite a long time, so that he now had no more than a bare ten minutes left for the following fourteen moves. This naturally signified for me a considerable relief. Even though I could not do anything active, still it was not at all easy for my adversary to work out something like a winning plan since now the calculation of the many tactical possibilities would consume a certain amount of time. It was nevertheless disappointing for me that Bronstein now played the comparatively careful move

42. R – Q2!

It might be disputed as to whether White, from the objective point of view, has some stronger continuation at his disposal. But, having consideration to the time trouble, the text-move must be praised, since it prevents, once and for all, the capture on QB6, and Black is reduced to complete passivity. In such a situation White can make his remaining fourteen moves without any difficulty and this means in its turn that my chances rapidly diminish.

Now let us have a look at what would have happened had White captured the pawn by *42.* R × RP. After this Black could in fact win the exchange, since Black gains an important tempo by *42. ....* B × R; *43.* QP × B, Kt – B4. If now *44.* R – R5, then Black can place his Knight on the strong square Q5 after *44. ....* Kt – K3 and then put up a tough resistance with the exchange more. After *44.* R – R2, Black does not need to accept the fresh sacrifice of the exchange *44. ....* Kt – K3; *45.* R – Q2, Kt – Q5; *46.* R × Kt, even though this is scarcely very dangerous, but he can get down to an ending by *44. ....* R × KtP; *45.* Kt × QP, Q × Kt; *46.* B × R, Kt – K3 followed by *47. ....* Kt – Q5 with an end game that can hardly be lost. As can be seen, Bronstein had good grounds for despising the pawn on R5, but this cost him valuable minutes.

Also after *42.* Q – Kt6, *42.* Q – R7, or *42.* Q – QB3, Black can take the exchange and after *43.* QP × B, continue with *43. . . . .* Kt – B4. In the case of *42.* Q – QB3, this continuation attains its tactical justification after *44.* Kt × KP, Q – B3!, and after *42.* Q – R3 Black can quietly play *42. . . . .* Q – K2, since *43.* Kt × QP is, practically speaking, no threat on account of *43. . . . .* B × R. Into consideration comes *42.* P – B4, but this possibility will not indeed run away and *42.* R – Q2 is a useful preparatory move in any case.

42. . . . .   P – R4

Black can only wait.

43. R – Q1

White, to my horror, does not show signs of wishing to do anything concrete. For the moment he intends to make his remaining moves before the next time control without a noticeable change in the position. White can of course play in this fashion since Black is forced to remain passive all the time. Objectively considered, Bronstein obviously had here several ways at his disposal that would have decisively increased his advantage. It would seem that the simplest was *43.* Q – QB3! with the double threat of *44.* Kt × KP, or *44.* Kt × QP, and even *44.* P – B4. In that event Black's dour and continuous defence would have been of no avail and Bronstein would have been able to reap the really well-deserved fruits of his earlier excellent play.

We ought not to censure the text-move on these grounds however. This would be to have one's attention too closely glued to one purpose only, and it certainly does not generally pay to embark on decisive operations when in time trouble. Since Black cannot in any case do anything, White should quietly and calmly have made neutral moves until the time control and thereafter he would hardly have allowed a sure win to slip from his grasp.

THE ART OF THE MIDDLE GAME

43.	. . . .	K – Kt1
44.	K – Kt1	K – R2
45.	Q – R3	

Does the opponent, after all, mean to do something positive while still in time trouble? The only chance is to give him the opportunity of so doing, and with this aim the pawn on Q3 is to be sacrificed.

45.	. . . .	Q – K2
46.	Q × RP?	

At long last, after ten moves of difficult – even prospectless – defence, the opponent makes a mistake! Bronstein used up additional precious minutes in convincing himself that the pawn-winning variation 46. Kt × QP, B × R; 47. QP × B, Kt × Kt leads to a position in which it is not so easy to force a win, e.g. 48. Q × Kt, Q × Q; 49. R × Q, P – R6; 50. R – Q2, (50. B – B4, P – R7; 51. R – Q1, allows 51. . . . . R × BP!) 50. . . . . R – R2, or 48. R × Kt, R – Q1; 49. R – Q3, Q × Q; 50. R × Q, R– Q5 followed eventually by R – Kt5 and the approach of the King. And now, when he has only a few minutes left, Bronstein suddenly loses his head and plunges into complications that he is far from being in a position to master. In the end, his opponent's dour resistance has obtained results.

Obviously, White could in fact have continued to play a waiting game. With this in mind, 46. Q – QB3 would have been very good, a move which, in addition, revives the threat of 47. Kt × KP.

46.	. . . .	Kt – B4

The value of the QRP was scarcely worth so much as to compensate the surrender of this tempo which is vitally important. Now suddenly Black obtains good counter-play and is in consequence at once relieved of all his burdens.

Keres

46

Bronstein

47. Q – B2

One misfortune seldom comes alone. White protects a comparatively worthless pawn and now gets the disadvantage in the end. A much better chance was *47.* Q – R5, since after *47.* ....
B × R; *48.* QP × B, Kt × P White, by *49.* B – B3! could have obtained a position in which his passed pawns would have become a really powerful factor. Black, of course, should not go in for the win of a pawn. He could have played the stronger *47.* .... R – R2 without first taking the exchange. If the Queen then retreated to QKt4, then the highly disagreeable *48.* ....
R – R7 could follow and after any other Queen moves the pawn on K4 could be captured without risk. We will not, however, discuss this position any longer since a more exact analysis is unimportant for us. The fact remains that Black has already surmounted all his difficulties.

47. ....   B × R!

And now the longed-for moment has come when Black can grasp the offered exchange without risk.

48. QP × B   R × KtP!

White had counted on this capture being impossible and now, despite everything, it happens, and, into the bargain, it comes just when he is in the worst time trouble. In the knowledge that

121

he has had a clearly won game and now has thrown it away the hapless Bronstein loses his self-confidence, and in the ensuing part of the game succumbs without a struggle.

In addition it should be noted that here Black might have made the grave oversight of *48.* .... Kt – K3; *49.* Kt – K3!, Kt – Q5; *50.* R × Kt, P × R; *51.* Kt – Q5, Q – Q1; *52.* P – Kt6! and White wins.

49. Kt × QP

If Bronstein had obtained this position after the normal development of a game it is to be supposed that, despite his grave time trouble, he would not have disdained the continuation *49.* Kt – K3!, R – Kt1; *50.* Kt – Q5, Q – Q1; *51.* Kt × R, Q × Kt, by which he would have obtained an equal game without much trouble. He deems himself, however, permanently obliged to achieve something concrete, and that in a position where in reality he should have tried to maintain the equilibrium. It is always difficult to adjust oneself psychologically to the true nature of affairs when one has played away the win. And naturally it is also unexpected when one suddenly obtains chances in a bad position. Therefore I am well-nigh convinced that had I now received the offer of a draw from Bronstein I would have accepted it.

49. ....   R – Kt3

Perhaps, in his time trouble, Bronstein had only reckoned with *49.* .... R – R4; *50.* Q – B3, with the further continuation *50.* .... R × P; *51.* Q × R, R × Kt and a probably drawn ending. The text-move, which is based on a tactical trick, must have come as a severe surprise to him. It is therefore easily understood that, without sufficient time on his clock, he should have missed his last chance.

50. B – Kt5?

The decisive mistake. The point of Black's last move lies in the fact that *50.* Q × Kt is followed by R(B2) × P whereupon White apparently loses the Knight and comes down to a difficult ending. But precisely in this variation there still lies a resource for White: *51*. Q × R(Kt6), R × Q; *52*. Kt – B8, Q – B4; *53*. Kt × R, Q × Kt and, with a careful defence, White could have held the ending. But to find this all out White, of necessity, required a little time, and this is exactly what was lacking at the moment.

50. ....   Kt – K3

Now the colossal threat of *51*. .... Kt – Q5 eventually wins further material. The struggle is already over.

51. B – R4

A longer resistance would have been put up by *51*. Q – B4, Kt – Q5; *52*. Q – Q5, but this would in no way have altered the result. After *52*. .... Kt × B; *53*. Kt × Kt, R × P Black wins the end game without difficulty. But now matters go even easier.

51. ....   Kt – Q5
52. Q – B5   R(Kt3) × P!

The last finesse. For the Rook Black not only obtains White's minor pieces but also his BP and that is more than enough.

53. B × R   R × B

Here the game ended as White was unable to make his three remaining moves before the time control. The flag on his clock fell and the game was therefore lost for him. He was in any case hopelessly placed as he had to lose the Knight as well.

The reader may perhaps think that this problem has little to do with the problem of defence and that here it is a question of a clear case of tournament luck. Of course he is right, since the position at the outset was from the purely chess point of view very bad for Black. Yes; in fact so bad that not even the most resourceful defence should have been sufficient. Objectively considered then Black could not hope for anything more than a loss.

The question becomes different when one regards it from the standpoint that the position is a phase in a struggle between two personalities. The one player has already practically lost the fight but he defends himself desperately and it is not so easy to give him the *coup de grâce*. And the longer one is able to put up a resistance, by continually setting the enemy new positional problems, the greater are the prospects of an eventually successful outcome to the game. Moreover, the opponent may also make a mistake and then we have indeed the aforementioned luck. This however will not come by itself. Good luck will go only to the player who contests a game in the right manner and thereby fashions for himself future possibilities. Hundreds of such examples are to be found in chess literature, even among the world's leading masters, and to ascribe all these to pure chance is in my opinion to treat the problem much too lightly.

With this example I must close my consideration of the problem of defence. It has not been intended as a systematic examination of all the problems that are bound up with defence; its only purpose is to serve as a guide by the aid of some examples to direct attention to a part of the struggle in chess which is of such great importance. My examples have fulfilled their purpose if they can influence the reader to a more timely conception of the importance of a skilful defence.

4

VARIOUS PAWN POSITIONS IN THE CENTRE

A. Kotov

Chess is often compared with war. In the one as in the other, rules exist for strategy and tactics: the combat is carried out in both cases in accordance with all the rules of the same art – mobilization, attack and defence, and manoeuvres. The nature of the topography plays a very important role in all army campaigns. If this is open, then the contest assumes the character of deep, encircling manoeuvres, or powerful, storming attacks, and if these are difficult to attain then one goes over to raids in depth on the flanks.

The placing of the centre pawns determines the 'topography' of a game of chess. On their exact arrangement depend equally the nature of the struggle and the tempo of the attacker's offensive. If, for instance, the centre is blocked by pawns then the pieces can only approach the opponent's camp by the aid of a deep encircling movement from the flanks. But if there are no pawns in the centre at all then such long-distance pieces as, for instance, Rooks and Bishops bombard enemy positions from their own bases.

Consequently, when one wants to sketch out one's plan of play and determine the character and tempo of the contest, then one is forced to give careful heed to the pawn position in the centre. Should one for example try to carry out an encircling flank attack when the centre is wide open, then the opponent may anticipate the attack by choosing a method of attack with direct bayonet-like thrusts.

In this chapter we shall make an attempt to elucidate the important question of pawn positions in the centre and the manner of play that is appropriate to each formation.

We shall study five main types of pawn positions in the centre, as follow.

1. The closed centre. Each player's pawns are locked with the other's, thus blocking the lines for Bishops and Rooks.

2. The open centre. There are no pawns in the centre and the lines and diagonals are free for the play of the pieces.

3. The mobile centre. One side has two or more united pawns in the centre and endeavours to advance them.

4. The fixed centre. The position of the pawns in the centre is in one way or another fixed and it is not easy to alter their position.

5. The dynamic centre. The pawn position in the centre is not fixed. It may be perhaps built up in some particular way and the resulting position then transposes to one of the positions we have described above.

A player must choose some kind of plan of play entirely in accordance with the type of pawn centre. To determine where an attack should be set in motion, how it should be conducted, and how the defence should be organized, all these procedures must in the first place fit in with the special conditions that are valid for the middle game with particular reference to the different formations of centre pawns.

We shall endeavour to determine the distinctive lines and examine the ways in which in practice chess masters in their games pay heed to the various factors that pertain to different pawn groupings in the centre.

I. THE CLOSED CENTRE

When both players have many pawns in the centre and these as it were hinge on each other, then we term this a closed centre. No lines exist along which the Rooks may operate; Bishop diagonals are blocked by either the enemy or their own pawns. Nor does there exist any hope that lines or diagonals will be opened in the near future. There remains therefore only one way out – play on the flanks. Usually the one player tries to open up the game on the wings and develop complicated and far-sighted plans of attack. The other side then has a number of ways from which to choose. What they are we will attempt to demonstrate by means of practical examples.

As is well known, the principle is this: when one has an advantage one must attack willy-nilly, otherwise the risk is that this advantage may disappear. In positions with a closed centre it is usually a question of an advantage on the wings. It is there that an attacker tends to be superior in matters of space, powers of mobility, and numbers of pawns. To utilize his advantage, the attacker must advance these pawns until the lines are opened up and breaches have been made by an assault with the major pieces.

The opponent can in this case organize his defence passively by lying in wait for the adversary's pawns and preventing his pieces from ensconcing themselves in their positions, even if the lines are opened up. But there also exists another type of game. That consists in quickly organizing a powerful counter-attack on the opposite wing. This counter-thrust completely diverts the opponent's forces and compels him to suspend his offensive on the other side of the board for a time, short or long.

Sometimes it is necessary to set in motion a counter-attack in the centre. With a closed centre this happens most often by a piece sacrifice, with the aim of breaking down the pawn position; or else it may be done by blasting it with the aid of one or more pawns. An attacker must be careful to maintain a watch on such counter-thrusts *since a counter-attack in the centre is the most effective answer to all the blows of a flank attack.*

Look at the following example in which the defence is astutely lying in wait for the enemy pawns that are attacking on the wings.

Nimzovich

47

Janowski

The position occurred in a tournament game at St Petersburg, 1914, between Janowski and Nimzovich. White intends to advance his pawns on the King's wing and thus exploit the fact that the centre is closed. It is interesting to follow the play and see how skilfully Nimzovich prevents this by building up blockade posts for the defence in the way of the White pawns.

1.	Kt – R2
2. P – KR4	Kt – B3
3. B – Q3	R – Kt1

Black anticipates in good time the dangerous advance, P – B4, by White. While White makes ready for the pawn storm by mobilizing his forces on the back lines, Black brings up reserves for the defence – this Rook is destined for K2. In so doing he threatens very conveniently to open up the QKt file by P – QKt4.

4. Q – K2	

Janowski also creates a defensive post – on Kt5. After *4*. .... Q – Q2 there would follow *5*. P – R4 when *5*. .... Q × P fails against *6*. R – R1.

4.	R – Kt2
5. B – B1	R(Kt2) – K2
6. K – R1	

Janowski has realized that for the present he cannot play P – B4 and he prepares to advance the Kt pawn. But Nimzovich is on the qui vive and swiftly fashions a new defensive point on his KKt5.

6.	B – B1
7. R – Kt1	K – B1
8. P – R5	Kt – R1
9. P – Kt4	Kt – R2
10. B – B2	

Most unwise would be *10*. P – Kt5, P × P; *11*. B × P, P – B3; *12*. B – B1, Kt – B2; *13*. P – R6, P – KKt4.

| 10. . . . . | R – Kt2 |
| 11. P – B4 | P – B3 |

Black enjoys a quadruple protection of the KKt4 square and it is risky for White to play immediately *12.* P – Kt5, RP × P; *13.* P × KtP, Kt × P; *14.* B × Kt, P × B after which his own King's position could also be broken up. Janowski proceeds to force exchanges after having first convinced himself that Black's position is proof against assault.

12. P × P	QP × P
13. Kt – B3	Kt – B2
14. R(Kt1) – B1	K – Kt1
15. Kt – R4	Kt – Q3
16. Kt – B5	B × Kt
17. KtP × B	Kt – KKt4
18. B × Kt	RP × B
19. B – R4	R – B1
20. B – B6	R – Kt1
21. P – R4	

And after some further developments, the game ended in a draw. The remaining moves are without interest as an illustration of our theme.

Yet another example. The diagram position occurred in the historic game between Alekhine and Capablanca (A.V.R.O., 1938) which was played on the Cuban master's fiftieth birthday.

Capablanca

48

Alekhine

The centre is closed. It is interesting to observe that the only file that is open, the QB file, has no importance or bearing on the result, since neither side can make use of it.

Capablanca, on his last move, transferred the Knight to KB2 so as to prepare the pawn attack on the King's wing by P – Kt4 followed by the further transference of the Knight to Kt3. How Alekhine prevents the carrying out of this plan has its own particular interest.

1. Q – Q2!

Now the move P – KKt4 is impossible. But, nevertheless, Black still wants to advance his KKt pawn.

1.	....	P – R3
2.	P – R4	Kt – R2
3.	P – R5!	

A decisive move. It is true that now Black has scope for his cavalry which can trot to Kt4 and K5, but in compensation Alekhine has the important point KKt6 and can set in motion an attack along the diagonal QKt1 – KR7.

3.	....	Kt(B2) – Kt4
4.	Kt – R4	Kt – K5
5.	Q – Kt2	K – B2

Black would be only too glad to do away with the dangerous Knight on KR4. But even after 5. .... B × Kt; 6. P × B, the Knight on K4 is without any square of retreat and sooner or later it will be lost.

6. P – B3

Black has completely failed to construct any safe shield against White's pawns and pieces. Alekhine demolishes his only point of defence on KB4, whereafter the White pieces attack the enemy King with unprecedented force.

6.	....	Kt(K5) – Kt4
7.	P – Kt4	P × P
8.	B – Kt6 ch	

The most exact sequence of moves. The King's retreat to the back rank shuts in the Black Rook on KR1 for ever.

| 8. .... | K – Kt1 |
| 9. P – B4 | Kt – B6? |

A seemingly inconsiderable error which Alekhine elegantly refutes. On KB6 the Knight is bereft of retreating possibilities and is doomed to destruction. But it is dubious if Black after the more correct 9. .... Kt – B2; 10. B – Q3 could have escaped from his most difficult position.

10. B × Kt ch!	R × B
11. Kt – Kt6	B – Q1
12. QR – QB1	

The only occasion on which White has needed the open file. Alekhine wants to have control of the only file for the Rooks for safety's sake.

| 12. .... | B – K1 |
| 13. K – Kt3! | |

Capablanca

49

Alekhine

The White King decides to deal personally with the impudent Knight that has so boldly swaggered into his domain. The enemy turns out to be too weak to accomplish anything serious and he is forced to watch helplessly whilst his bold but fool-hardy cavalier perishes.

13.	Q – KB2
14. K × P	Kt – R5
15. Kt × Kt	Q × RP ch
16. K – Kt3	Q – B2
17. Kt – KB3	P – R4

Here Capablanca exceeded the time limit, but his position is hopeless in any case.

The next example is most instructive for its correct insight into the importance of the centre. It is from the game Kotov–Spassky (U.S.S.R. Championship, Riga, 1958).

Spassky

50

Kotov

The centre is completely blocked by the pawns of both players. The plan of play is obvious: White will set his pawns into motion on the King's wing, Black on the Queen's side. Which will get there first? The answer to this question is decisive in a marked degree for the outcome of the game.

Black has not succeeded in establishing points of defence to impede the way of the White pawns. But this is not a vital necessity, as becomes clear in the course of play. White can open up the KR file, but is not in a position to use this effectively enough.

Black in his turn will advance his pawns on the Queen's side and, should the occasion arise, will sacrifice one of them. The struggle is nicely balanced and it is full of interesting moments.

1. B – Q3	P – QKt4
2. Q – Q2	

Fair or foul, the pawn should have been taken. It is true that now the game runs along approximately the same lines after an exchange of pawns, but the material is level.

2.	P × P
3. KB × P	

But here it was absolutely necessary to give up the pawn. After *3.* B – QB2 Black would have experienced much more difficulty in developing his offensive on the Queen's side.

3.	Kt – Q2
4. P – R5	Kt – Kt3
5. B – Q3	P – R4
6. P × P	BP × P
7. Q – R2	Kt – B3
8. Kt – R3	Q – K2
9. Kt – K2?	

A dubious manoeuvre. White overestimates the strength of the pawns' anchorage in the centre and soon gets into difficulties. If he had played *9.* K – Q2, and then *10.* QR – KKt1, possibilities would have arisen of setting into motion a King-side attack. But now his position becomes bad.

9.	R – Kt1
10. Kt – Kt3	P – B5
11. B – QB2	

Spassky

Kotov

11. ....   Kt(Kt3) × P!

Brilliant positional judgement! The White King is fixed in the centre and White's pieces have been induced by the attack on the King's side to abandon their control of the centre. The piece sacrifice at once opens up lines for the Black pieces, which hurl themselves against the enemy King with terrific force.

'The best answer to a flank attack is a counter-thrust in the centre' – in the heat of the fight White forgets this rule and for this his opponent punishes him grievously. The pawn centre that seemed impenetrable a moment ago now no longer impedes Black's pieces. The game assumes an open character and the pawn structure passes from one type to another.

> *12.* P × Kt   R × P
> *13.* Kt – Kt5   P – R3?

Unpardonably careless. Hardly has Black opened up the position than he gives his opponent the opportunity of closing it. The explanation of Spassky's unfortunate move must be simply that he has quite miscalculated his analysis of the position. After the correct *13.* .... P – K5! all Black's pieces would have come into play and White would have been in a critical situation. Now, instead, he suddenly begins to find himself in a winning one!

134

14. Kt(Kt5) – K4!	Kt × QP
15. B × P	

Likewise careless. First he should have prepared this move by driving away the Rook from Kt2 by *15.* B – B1, and then he should have captured the pawn.

15.	Kt – Kt5
16. B – Kt5	Q – QB2?

A mistake that spoils the game. After the correct *16.* .... Kt × B ch; *17.* Q × Kt, Q – Kt2 Black would have had an enduring and dangerous initiative. Now the White pieces proceed to harry the Black King.

17. Q – R7 ch	K – B2
18. R – R6!	

Spassky had failed to reckon with this strong move. With the fall of the KKt pawn all Black's defensive bulwarks break down and his King falls victim to an irresistible attack.

18.	Kt × B ch
19. K – B1	Kt – Q5
20. Q × P ch	K – Kt1
21. Q – R7 ch	K – B2
22. Kt × P ch	Q × Kt
23. R × Q	Kt – K3
24. Kt – B5	R – R1
25. Kt – R6 ch	resigns.

Now let us make a brief summary of it all. In positions where the centre is closed play must proceed slowly and is always situated on the flanks. The player who is attacked organizes a counter-attack on the other wing and at the same time he constructs special obstructions to impede the oncoming infantry. As quickly as the opportunity allows a counter-attack in the centre must be carried out, almost always in conjunction with a sacrifice, so as to get at the enemy King which eventually will be left in the lurch by its own pieces under the pressure of the attack.

II. THE OPEN CENTRE

In this type, which provides a clear contrast to the previous one, there are in the centre either no pawns or else one only, and that one of very little importance. As to characterizing this position, whereas in the previous examples the 'topography' of the centre offered an abundance of impenetrable forests, barricades, and marshes, the open pawn centre reminds one of an even plain. While the former required encircling manoeuvres from the flanks, now it is a question of bold cavalry charges, and of powerful storming attacks with whole armies. It is interesting to observe that in the dawn of chess history, in the time of Morphy and Anderssen, the open centre was always the objective aimed at. Then players were fond of the direct bayonet attack without artful manoeuvres or roundabout ways. Only with the coming of Steinitz did play in closed positions win many adherents.

How should one proceed when the opponent's centre becomes an open one? We will deal here with the question both from the point of view of the attacking and the defending side.

The attacking side usually tries to conjure up weaknesses in the opponent's position by piece play and then to attack these vulnerable points. Usually, too, no pawn storms occur, since a pawn weakness in one's own position becomes very risky once the centre is open. It must be added that the offensive should only be carried out when and where the attacker has a clear advantage.

The defence aims at warding off the opponent's attack, while avoiding as much as possible weaknesses in the pawn position. In the best of these cases the defence itself goes over to the counter-attack, or else exploits the opponent's excessively bold play to gain a material advantage.

Here is an example of play in the open pawn centre. The position arose in a celebrated game between Alekhine and Emanuel Lasker (Zurich, 1934).

Lasker

52

Alekhine

White has his pieces posted actively for attack on the King's wing. To begin with, Alekhine creates a weakness in the pawn structure shielding Black's King.

    1. Q – Q6   Kt(K4) – Q2

Bad is *1.* .... Kt – Kt3; *2.* Kt – R6 ch, P × Kt; *3.* Q × Kt, Q – Q1; *4.* Q – QB3, when Black's King's side is weakened beyond repair.

    2. R(KB1) – Q1   R(R1) – Q1
    3. Q – Kt3   P – Kt3

The first objective has been attained. The weakness that has been created gives White an opportunity of noticeably strengthening his piece attack.

    4. Q – Kt5!   K – R1

Otherwise there follows R – Q4 – KR4, or else even *5.* R – Q6.

    5. Kt – Q6   K – Kt2
    6. P – K4   Kt – KKt1
    7. R – Q3   P – B3

This fresh, and practically forced, weakness results in an elegant finish. Curiously enough, almost the same mate would

have followed after 7. .... P – R3; 8. Kt – B5 ch, K – R2;
9. Kt × P, P – B3; 10. Kt – B5!, P × Kt; 11. R – R3 ch, Kt –
R3; 12. R × Kt mate.

8. Kt – B5 ch	K – R1
9. Q × P!	resigns.

There is no defence against the mate on Kt2, or, if the Queen
is taken, against mate by R – R3. This historic position deserves
a diagram.

Lasker

53

Alekhine

Now let us examine another example on the same theme.

Vaitonis

54

Szabo

The diagram position is from the game Szabo–Vaitonis (Saltsjöbaden, 1952). There are no pawns in the centre (those on the respective K3s play no role in practice). White's pieces are more actively placed. This affords Szabo the possibility of at once setting into motion an onslaught on the weak points in Black's position.

But where are the weak points? It is not so easy for the reader to discern that the most vulnerable point in the Black King's castled position is KB2. White's ensuing energetic manoeuvre unveils this weakness.

1.	Kt – B5 !	Q – B1
2.	Kt – Q6	QR – Kt1
3.	Kt – KKt5	Kt – Kt5

3. .... B – B1 would have offered better defensive chances since now White breaks to pieces the main bulwark of Black's defence by a piece sacrifice.

4.	Q – Kt3	Kt – R3
5.	Kt(Q6) × BP	Kt × Kt
6.	B × P	B – K1

It will not do to capture the Bishop: 6. .... B × B; 7. Kt × B, and the Queen is lost.

7.	R – B7	R – Q2

Or 7. .... Kt – Q2; 8. Kt × Kt, B × Kt; 9. B × Kt.

8.	R × R	Kt × R
9.	R – Q1	Q – K2

The move 9. .... R – Q1 is bad: 10. Q – B7, Q – K2; 11. Kt × Kt, B × Kt; 12. R × Kt, R × R; 13. B × R, and White wins. But neither is it at all difficult to win now.

10.	R × Kt	R – Q1
11.	R × R	Q × R
12.	P – KR3	

And so White won two pawns and had no difficulty in converting this advantage into a win.

We shall now quote an original example from the same tournament. It is true that White's centre pawn is of importance here, but this does not have a marked bearing on our appraisal of the position.

Matanovic

55

Kotov

This position occurred in the game Kotov–Matanovic. White takes advantage of his opponent's positional weaknesses by some complicated manoeuvres.

    1. QR – Kt1

This forces the QKt pawn to advance, and thus weakens Black's QB3.

1.	P – Kt3
2. Kt – B3	Q – Q1
3. Q – B4	R – B1
4. P – K4	R – QR4
5. Kt – K5	

White is obsessed by his idea and does not observe the clear winning method by *5.* KR – Q1 with either *6.* Kt – K5 or *6.* Kt – Kt5 to follow, But it is an ill wind that blows nobody good and the remainder of the game offers something quite extra in compensation.

5. . . . .   P – B3 !

Brilliant defensive play. After *6.* Kt – Kt4, there would follow *6. . . . .* P – K4 !

6. Kt × B	Q × Kt
7. Q × P	R – B1
8. Q – R6	R × RP
9. R – Kt3	Q – K2

A Rook check on Kt3 was threatened. White's win depends on whether he can arrive at P – K5 or P – KB4.

10. R – Kt3 ch	K – R1
11. P – K5	R – R5
12. Q – B1 !	

From here the Queen can coordinate the operations of the remaining pieces. Now *13.* P – B4 is threatened when the Black Rook on KR5 would be shut out of the game.

12.	R(R5) – KB5
13. R – QB3	P – QR4
14. R – B7	Q – Kt5
15. Q – K3	

White does not allow himself to be lured into the pretty trap of *15.* R – Q1, R × P; *16.* Q – R6, R – B8 ch!; *17.* R × R, Q – Q5 ch with a won game for Black.

15.	P – R5
16. P – Kt3	R(B5) – B2
17. R – B6	R – QKt2
18. R × KP	P – R6

A dangerous pawn; but White also has a passed pawn on K5, and its advance can be combined with a King-side attack.

19. R – KB6	R – R1
20. P – K6	Q – Kt7

He was threatened with the unpleasant *21.* Q – K5.

21. Q – KB3   R – KKt1
22. R – B8!   R – R2

Black does not choose the best defensive move and thus deprives White of the opportunity of demonstrating an interesting way of winning. After the correct 22. .... R(Kt2) – Kt2 the win would be obtained in quite fantastic style by 23. R – Q1, P – R7; 24. P – K7, P – R8 = Q; 25. P – K8 = Q, Q(R8) – R7; 26. R – Q8, Q(R7) – Kt6; 27. Q – R8, Q(Kt7) – R7.

Matanovic

56

Kotov
(Variation)

In this position, which would appear to be unique in chess history, White wins by exchanging off all the eight (!) pieces on KKt8 and also by 28. R × R ch, Q × R; 29. Q × Q, or 28. .... R × R; 29. Q – K5 mate.

23. R × R ch   K × R
24. Q – Q5!   resigns.

Let us summarize our conclusions. In positions where the centre is open play with the pieces takes place; on the other hand, as a rule, no pawn attacks, since pawn advances expose one's own King. The attacker tries to create weaknesses in the enemy position and to exploit these to obtain either a mating attack or else decisive material advantage. The defence attempts to ward off the enemy attack and then to go over to the counter-attack. Sometimes one can utilize the attacker's rashness or fool-hardy taking-of-chances to obtain material superiority.

Before we pass on to the next type of pawn formation we shall discuss the question of the changing from one pawn formation to another. It is quite apparent that a position with an open pawn centre cannot transpose to a position with a closed centre – where can the pawns come from? But the opposite process is possible, though it occurs but seldom. Sometimes it happens that the players both exchange off all their centre pawns and the closed centre breaks up. In this way it is theoretically possible to bring about changes from closed to open centres.

III. THE MOBILE CENTRE

When one side has a pawn chain in the centre containing at the very least two united pawns, this may constitute a marked advantage. In those cases where one's opponent is entirely without centre pawns or has only one pawn there, then we term the centre a mobile one.

How should one play in positions where the pawn centre is mobile? The side that has the centre pawns (naturally we are not speaking of the case where the pawns in the centre are weak and must be defended) usually tries to advance them and establish one or two passed pawns in the centre, which may well decide the issue of the game. But it is not always possible to succeed in realizing so ideal a plan of operations. More often it happens that the side that controls the centre forces away the enemy pieces from the fine central squares with the aid of his pawns and then transfers the attack to the wings where it may prove decisive.

The plan of play for the defence consists in trying either to check or block the enemy pawns. This is the first problem. Then the scheme is to undermine or destroy the centre. A pawn centre usually prevents the defence from organizing counter-play on the wings. All one's attention must be concentrated on the centre.

We shall present an example of such a struggle by choosing the ending of the game Konstantinopolsky–Kotov (U.S.S.R. Championship, 1945).

Kotov

Konstantinopolsky

White has but one method of obtaining active play. This consists in creating a mobile pawn centre by P – B3 and P – K4. In such cases the pawns on Q4 and K4, supported by the two Bishops, can advance and beat back the enemy pieces.

Black seeks to delay the advance of the White pawns by gradually blocking them or else even liquidating them.

1.	R – K1	B – B1

The first attempt at restraining the pawn on White's K3 – the Bishop is destined for B4.

2.	P – B3	Kt × Kt
3.	B × Kt	B – B4
4.	Q – Q2	P – KR4

Black wishes to prevent P – KKt4 and intends to play P – R5 eventually.

5.	R – K2	Q – Q2!

A far-sighted move. Black cannot prevent the K pawn from advancing, and therefore intends to let it come on as far as K5 and then to blockade the opponent's centre pawns on the Q4 and K3 squares. Therefore, too, he must exchange off the Bishop on white-coloured squares.

6. QR – K1	B – R6
7. B – KR1	R – K3
8. P – K4	P × P
9. P × P	QR – K1
10. B – B3	

Black was threatening *10.* .... B – Kt5; *11.* R – K3, Q – K2; *12.* Q – Q3, Kt – Q4.

10.	B – Kt5
11. Q – B4	B × B
12. Q × B	Q – K2
13. P – K5	

This was forced. Now White's pawns are blocked. In addition, White has an impotent Bishop that moves on squares that, for the most part, are blocked by its own pawns.

13.	Kt – Q4
14. B – Q2	

And here Black continued *14.* .... Q – R6 which resulted in dangerous complications because of White's attack on the point KB7. Instead he should have played *14.* .... P – R5! with an excellent game.

Yet another example in which Black succeeded in checking the advance of his opponent's pawn centre.

The position in the diagram is from the game Reshevsky-Botvinnik (A.V.R.O. 1938).

Botvinnik

58

Reshevsky

This position has come from play on well-known theoretical paths; now Reshevsky intends to advance his centre pawns. He therefore develops his Bishop on KKt2.

1. P – KKt3	Kt – Q2
2. B – Kt2	Kt – B3

Botvinnik also devotes all his attention to the centre. The Knight on KB3 prevents the advance of the pawn to K4.

3. O – O	B – Q3
4. Kt – B3	P – B3
5. P – QKt4?	

Reshevsky takes the wrong path. He should have at once played 5. Q – Q3, with the further continuation of P – B3 and P – K4. The American master's attempt to combine the attack in the centre with a strengthening of the position on the Queen's wing gives Botvinnik an opportunity of seizing the initiative.

5.	P – QR3
6. R – K1	R – K1
7. B – Kt2	B – B1
8. Q – Q3	B – K3
9. P – B3	Kt – Q2 !

A subtle retort. Now, in reply to 10. P – K4, there would follow 10. .... P × P; 11. P × P, Kt – K4; 12. Q – Q1, B – KKt5; 13. Kt – K2, Kt –B6 ch; 14. B × Kt, B × B; 15. P – K5, Q – Kt4 or Q – Kt3 with considerable advantage to Black.

10. Kt – R4	P – QKt3 !

Once again an excellent move by Botvinnik. He does not reveal his plans but waits for White to play QR – B1.

11. QR – B1	P – QKt4
12. Kt – B5	Kt – Kt3
13. B – B3	R – R2

Botvinnik continues to pursue the right policy, and prevents the advance P – K4 by all possible means. The Rook is placed so as to be ready to traverse the second rank and reach the file where it can be of the greatest use.

14.	P – K4	Kt – B5
15.	R – R1	B × Kt!
16.	QP × B	R – Q2!

White's situation has become critical. Nothing remains of his pawn centre and he must now concern himself with the defence of his weak central position.

17.	Q – Q4	P – B3
18.	P – B4	P × P
19.	Q × KP	R – Q6
20.	QR – B1	R × B!
21.	R × R	B – B2
22.	R – Q3	

Botvinnik

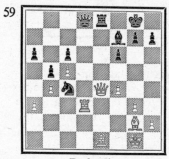

59

Reshevsky

Here Botvinnik played the faulty 22. .... Q – Kt1? and his resourceful opponent succeeded in obtaining a draw. The simple 22. .... Q – B1!, on the other hand, would have won easily, e.g. 23. KR – Q1, R × Q; 24. B × R, B – Q4!, 25. B × B ch, P × B; 26. R × P, Q – K3; 27. P – B5, Q – K6 ch; and P – KR4.

It was on purpose that we commenced by discussing those positions in which the defending side succeeded in holding back the attacking thrusts of the White pawns. Alas for those who have not taken measures in good time to hold them back! Uncontrollable centre pawns can easily drive all protecting forces right out of the way and spread panic and terror in the enemy ranks.

The game Kotov–Unzicker (Saltsjöbaden, 1952) may be quoted as an example of a triumph of this kind for a pawn chain in the centre.

Unzicker

60

Kotov

White at once starts to build up a mobile pawn centre. Black, who has failed to take preventive measures beforehand, can do nothing against the enemy attack in the centre.

1. P – B3   Kt – Kt1

The intention is to play this piece to B3, but better defensive possibilities would have been offered by *1.* .... Kt – B2 and *2.* .... Kt – K3.

   2. Q – Q3   R – K1
   3. Kt – Kt3   Kt – B3
   4. B – Kt2   R – QB1
   5. QR – K1   P – KR3

Black makes room for the Knight on R2. But this is hardly the way to deal effectively with White's pawn offensive. By *5.* .... P – B5; *6.* Q – B2, P – QKt4; *7.* P – K4, P – Kt3; *8.* P – K5,

148

Kt – Q2; 9. P – B4, P – B4 Black could have prevented any further advance in the centre.

6.	P – K4	BP × P
7.	BP × P	P × P
8.	P × P	Kt – K4
9.	Q – Q1	Kt – B5
10.	B – B1	

Black is lost; he has no means of opposing White's powerful centre. Furthermore, there exist most dangerous threats on the King's wing, and Black cannot protect the points KKt2 and KR3.

10.	....	Kt – R2
11.	P – K5	R – K3
12.	R – K4	

Now White's game plays itself. He can at his leisure and in all quiet concentrate his forces for the decisive storming of the King's wing.

12.	....	Kt – B1
13.	Kt – B5	K – R1
14.	Q – R5	R – B2
15.	R – R4	Kt – R2
16.	Kt × KtP!	

A simple sacrifice that destroys all Black's bulwarks of defence on the King's wing.

16.	....	K × Kt
17.	B × P ch	K – Kt1
18.	R – Kt4 ch	R – Kt3
19.	P – K6!	resigns.

Let us sum up. In positions with mobile pawn centres everything depends on the following question. Can the defender prevent the attacker's pawns from advancing and can he blockade them? If he can then this would signify an outstanding success. After he has stopped the centre from advancing the defender can even begin to think of how he can most suitably demolish it. But once the pawn centre breaks loose or can move freely then the hope of saving the game diminishes to a degree. Therefore, once the opponent has succeeded in establishing a pawn centre, then all measures to stop and block it must be taken in good time.

We will now consider a matter that is of importance in this connexion, namely the transformation of a position with a mobile pawn centre to one with a centre of another type.

By means of pawn exchanges in the centre, positions with an open centre can occur, and by retarding manoeuvres that slow down the game sometimes positions with closed centres can be created (even if these seldom arise). But more important is the opposite turn of events. A position with an open centre cannot, it is true, be transformed to one with a mobile centre (there are of course no pawns), but a position with a closed centre can easily be changed into one in which the pawns may suddenly advance. This often occurs after a sacrifice on the part of the attacker. By sacrificing a minor piece, or even, more rarely, a Rook, one side suddenly shatters a closed centre and obtains a position with mobile pawns. This way of play occurs quite often and must always be borne in mind.

See for example how brilliantly Euwe executes such a sacrifice in one of the games of his match with Alekhine in the year 1935 (twenty-sixth match game).

Alekhine

61

Euwe

The centre is closed, but with the aid of the sparkling sacrifice that now follows White's pawns are set in motion.

1.	Kt × P!	B × B
2.	Kt × QP	Q – Kt1
3.	Kt × P	B – B3
4.	Kt – Q2!	

With the unpleasant threat of P – K4 – K5. Alekhine tries to blunt the force of this advance.

4.	....	P – KKt4!
5.	P – K4	P × P
6.	P × P	B – Q5
7.	P – K5	Q – K1
8.	P – K6	R – KKt1

Black's pieces are bound down by his opponent's formidable central pawn chain. It is not surprising that Euwe rapidly obtains a decisive advantage, even though an inaccuracy does creep in.

9.	Kt – B3

Stronger would have been Q – KR3 with a number of dangerous threats.

9.	....	Q – Kt3
10.	R – KKt1	B × R
11.	R × B	Q – B3?

In his turn, Black commits an error. *11. .... Q – B4* was the right move.

12.	Kt – Kt5!	R – Kt2
13.	P × Kt	R × P
14.	Q – K3	R – K2
15.	Kt – K6	R – KB1
16.	Q – K5	Q × Q
17.	P × Q	R – B4

The end game is won for White, but it demands precise technique.

18.	R – K1	P – KR3
19.	Kt – Q8	R – B7
20.	P – K6	R – Q7
21.	Kt – B6	R – K1
22.	P – K7	P – Kt4
23.	Kt – Q8	K – Kt2
24.	Kt – Kt7	K – B3
25.	R – K6 ch	K – Kt4
26.	Kt – Q6	R × KP
27.	Kt – K4 ch	resigns.

IV. THE FIXED CENTRE

In this case the pawn position in the centre is held in a closely locked grip and cannot be changed unless extraordinary methods are employed (sacrifices and the sudden destruction that goes with these). Here the centre may consist of a pawn on each side, and usually these pawns are placed directly opposite each other. It should be observed that other central formations also may occur.

A fixed central position lends a special character to the play on both sides. The struggle may be concentrated in the centre, towards which, in such cases, both players will direct their pieces; but it may also take place on the wings when one of the players utilizes the relative stability in the centre to throw forward his pieces in a flank assault. Let us now consider how both players conduct the play in positions with fixed centres.

The attacking side stations his pieces in and around the centre, and occupies the central field to the greatest possible extent. Superiority in the centre gradually forces the opponent to yield and retire, and this in turn is the source of fresh positional and even material disadvantages. Sometimes the attacker can, by reason of his superiority in the centre, set in motion a successful flank attack. The defending side seeks to drive the enemy pieces away from the central field or to exchange them off. In both cases he lessens the opponent's pressure and at the same time prepares for an eventual wing attack. After he has beaten back the enemy's direct attack he can even begin to think of a counter-attack.

Positions with fixed centres demand great skill from the players. Botvinnik is wont to display phenomenal virtuosity in such positions and we will quote one of his games on this theme.

In the diagram position Botvinnik plays Black against M. Stolberg (U.S.S.R. Championship, 1940).

Botvinnik

Stolberg

In this position White wants to entrench his pieces on K5 and QB5, and Black seeks to do likewise on his K5 and QB5. As always, Botvinnik conducts the game logically and obtains a decisive advantage in a few moves.

　　1. . . . .　　　　　　　　　　　B – KB4 !

Exchange of Bishops makes it easier for Black to obtain control of the squares K5 and QB5.

　　2. Q – B2　　　　　　　　　　B – K5
　　3. P – Kt5

This move gives Black the opportunity of obtaining a firm hold of the vital QB5 square. *3. QR – Q1* would have been better.

3.	B × B
4. Q × B	Kt – QR4
5. Kt – Kt3	

Bad would be 5. Kt × P, Kt × Kt; 6. B × Kt, R – K6; with
strong pressure for Black.

5.	Kt – B5
6. B – B1	QR – B1
7. R – R2	B – B1
8. P – QR4	B – Kt5

Black takes the opportunity of reducing the number of White
pieces defending the K5 square.

9. Kt – Q1	Kt – K5

More exact would be 9. .... Kt – Q3 and 10. .... Kt – K5.
But the text-move is also sufficient.

10. P – B5	Kt × Kt
11. Q × Kt(Kt3)	B – Q3
12. Q – KB3	B – K2
13. Q – KKt3	B – B3
14. B × P	B × P ch
15. K – R1	P – B3

All in all, White has only one pawn, that on KB5, in the
centre, and this is an ill-boding symptom of the shape of things
to come.

16. B – B1	R – K5

All this time matters are concentrated on just this particular
outpost in the centre.

17. Q – Q3	Kt – K4
18. Q – Kt1	R – QB5

Now the centre has become a pleasant parking place for
nearly all Black's pieces.

19.	P – R5	B – B4
20.	P – Kt6	P – R3
21.	Kt – Kt2	R – B6
22.	B – Q2	R – QKt6
23.	Q – B2	Q – Kt4
24.	R – B1	B – B1
25.	R – Q1	R – K7

With the aid of centralization Black has been able to carry out an invasion of the opponent's camp with his major pieces. Now comes the decisive phase – the attack on the King.

26.	Q – B1	R × P ch!
27.	P × R	P – Q5
	White resigns.	

We will give yet another example of Botvinnik's method of play in positions with a fixed centre.

The diagram is taken from his game with Kotov in the 1941 U.S.S.R. Championship.

Botvinnik

Kotov

Taking everything into consideration White has the better position. The Black King has forfeited its chance of castling and his pieces on the King's wing are not yet developed. It is all the more instructive to see how skilfully Botvinnik utilizes such advantages as are to be found in his own position. By means of

155

a methodical centralization of his pieces he succeeds in over-hauling his opponent's advantage in development and eventu-ally gaining the initiative for himself.

1.	Q – Q3	Q – B1

The Queen is bound for K3 from where it can control both the important central squares of K5 and QB5.

2.	QR – B1	Q – K3
3.	B – Kt2	P – KR4
4.	Kt – K2	P – QKt4
5.	Kt – B4	

White decides to refrain from capturing on QB4 for fear of the threatening pawn mass on the Queen's wing after *5.* R × R, QP × R. But, nevertheless, this would have been the best course, since now the grip of the Black pieces on the squares QB5 and K5 render any active play on White's part impossible.

5.	....	Q – K2
6.	Q – Q1	P – R5
7.	Q – B3	

White finds it difficult to continue in any positive way and makes a waiting manoeuvre. Botvinnik meanwhile completes his development and brings up fresh reserves to fight in the centre.

7.	....	K – Kt1
8.	KR – Q1	Kt – K5
9.	Kt – Q3	R – R3
10.	Q – K2	P × P
11.	BP × P	Q – Kt4
12.	B × Kt	

White reckons on obtaining chances of saving the game with Bishops of opposite colour. But Botvinnik's subtle manoeuvres demonstrate exactly how the attack should be carried out in a position with Bishops of opposite colour.

12.	P × B
13. Kt – B4	B × Kt!
14. KP × B	Q – Q4!

Botvinnik

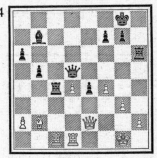

64

Kotov

The decisive move. White loses not only the pawn on QR2 but also any possibility of preventing the Black pieces from furiously assaulting his King. If the Queen now blockades the K pawn by *15.* Q – K3, then Black can capture the QR pawn by *15.* .... R × R; *16.* R × R, Q × RP; but he can also increase the pressure by *15.* ..... R(R3) – QB3.

15. Q – Kt2	R(R3) – QB3
16. R × R	R × R
17. P – KR3	P – Kt5
18. K – R2	P – K6!

Simple and decisive. White's answer is forced.

19. Q × Q	R – B7 ch
20. K – Kt1	B × Q
resigns.	

We have now considered positions with a fixed centre in which both players have pawns opposite each other. But other types of fixed centre come into consideration. In many games isolated centre pawns occur, e.g. when White has a pawn on Q4 and Black one only on his Q4. This is also a fixed centre, as any change would require radical measures which as a rule can be executed comparatively seldom.

Here is an example of the method of play in a position with an isolated QP. The diagram position occurred in a game between Botvinnik and Vidmar at Nottingham, 1936.

Vidmar

65

Botvinnik

White has an isolated pawn on Q4. It is, for all practical purposes, fixed, since White can hardly force the barrier of Black pieces that blockade Q5. But it would also be detrimental for White to free himself from the blockade on Q5 since this provides him with a trustworthy support for his pieces on an adjacent square. Again, we should closely study Botvinnik's manoeuvres here – they are typical of such positions.

1. Q – Q3!

With a twofold aim; to create a threat on KR7 by B – B2 and in addition to transfer the Queen to KR3 where it serves an important attacking purpose.

1. ....   Kt(Kt3) – Q4
2. Kt – K5

A safe and sure place for the Knight. On here it constitutes a dangerous threat to the KB7 point and it also supports the White pawns in their attacking efforts on the King's wing.

2.	....	B – B3
3.	QR – Q1	Kt – QKt5
4.	Q – R3	B – Q4

A grave error. Black should not squander his white-square Bishop; if it had to be exchanged, then it should have been for the Knight on K5. Botvinnik exploits his opponent's mistake in the most effective way.

5.	Kt × B	Kt(Kt5) × Kt
6.	P – B4 !	

Now the KB file is opened and Black's control of the Q4 point is weakened. In the ensuing phase of the game the White Bishop on QKt3 plays an important role. Hence Black should not have deprived himself of his Q Bishop which could have become a serious rival to White's Bishop on QKt3.

6.	....	R – B1

Black fails to defend his position in the best way. A tougher resistance would have been provided by 6. .... P – KKt3. Then it would have cost Botvinnik really great exertions to break down the enemy pawn chain on the King's side. After 6. .... P – KKt3; 7. B – R6, R – K1; 8. P – Kt4, White would however be in a position to carry out the inevitable move P – B5. It is interesting to observe that the energetic thrust P – KKt4 is made possible by Black's having exchanged off his Q Bishop. The reader will surely have already perceived how important the Bishop is for Black's defence in positions of this kind with isolated pawns.

7.	P – B5	P × P
8.	R × P	Q – Q3

This loses at once. Black could have put up a better resistance after 8. .... R – B2, but even then 9. R(Q1) – KB1 would be a difficult threat to parry.

Vidmar

66

Botvinnik

9. Kt × P!

Botvinnik is making use of the unsatisfactory placing of the Black pieces. Capturing the Knight with the King would be bad on account of 10. R × Kt (Q5).

| 9. .... | R × Kt |
| 10. B × KKt | B × B |

Or 10. .... Kt × B; 11. R × Kt, and 12. Q × R.

| 11. R × Kt | Q – B3 |
| 12. R – Q6! | |

White avoids the trap of 12. R – QB5?, B × P ch.

| 12. .... | Q – K1 |
| 13. R – Q7 | resigns. |

Summarizing our conclusions then: in positions with fixed centres play can develop along two different lines. The attacker may work for a methodical increase of his strength in the centre until he obtains a decisive advantage. An important method of achieving this is often by the liquidation of the enemy pawns protecting the central squares. When the attacker has in fact obtained command of the centre, then he can plan a break-through there, or else transfer the attack to the flank.

But another method is also used. The attacker at once

embarks upon play on the flanks and takes advantage of the fact that the centre is fixed and that the opponent cannot execute a decisive counter-thrust there. For this reason one should of course never neglect thinking about the centre, since safety there is a prerequisite for all kinds of flank attacks.

In both these cases the defending side lies in wait for the opponent's plan of attack to divulge itself and then commences operations on the other sector of the front so as to divert the enemy forces.

Let us now take up the question as to how positions with a fixed centre can be changed into central formations of another type.

By demolishing the opponent's pawns one can easily change the position from that of a fixed to a mobile central type, and if both players' pawns disappear then an open centre may arise. Alternatively, from positions with a closed centre, there can easily arise the type with fixed centres and even mobile centres may occur. A problem which demands particular care arises when the player who has the mobile centre must determine in what fashion it should be fixed. It is then that a player may get into great difficulties which demand the greatest playing skill.

Let us, for example, consider the following position from a game in the year 1935 between Lilienthal and Flohr. In this there occurs an interesting case of change in the centre.

Flohr

67

Lilienthal

In the position in the diagram Black exerts strong pressure on
K5. If White confines himself merely to defending the pawn
then he runs the risk of having the initiative taken out of his
hands. So he must do something about his pawn position
in the centre. But what? Why not play P – K5? (Such a move is
indeed playable at the appropriate time. In this connexion the
reader should study the game Kotov–Gligoric, Moscow, 1947.
But it should be observed that special positional circumstances
existed to justify the move.) Lilienthal finds an elegant solution
to the difficult problem.

1. P – Q5!		P × P
2. Kt – Q4!		

A remarkable move. Now he threatens the decisive 3. Kt –
B5 and 4. Q – Kt5. Quite suddenly Black's position takes on a
most unprepossessing appearance. White has opened up the
centre and has not only activated his Bishops but has also united
all his pieces for the attack in the ensuing moves.

2.		B – B4
3. P – K5		

Lilienthal wants to use his pawns for the attack, but in so
doing he allows his opponent the opportunity of organizing a
defence. Excellent winning chances would have been given by
3. R × B, P × R; 4. Kt – B5, P – Q5; 5. Q – Kt5.

3.		Kt – K5
4. P – B3		Q – K1!

Excellent! By means of the piece sacrifice Black obtains a
dangerous mobile centre supported by active forces.

5. P × Kt		Q × P
6. R – K1		R – K1

Now Black gains his third pawn for the Knight and thus, in
addition to everything else, he restores the balance in material.
White must in his turn strive for equality.

7. K – R1		P × P
8. B – B2		R – Q1

9. R – Q1	P – KR3
10. B – B3	P – B4

How is White to escape from the threatened attack by Black's mobile pawn centre? With the ensuing elegant manoeuvre Lilienthal solves the difficult problem in a combinational way.

Flohr

Lilienthal

11. R – Q2!

After 11. .... P – B5 there would now follow 12. Kt – K6!, R – K1 (12. .... R × R; 13. Q × R, Q × Kt?; 14. B – Kt3); 13. Q – R3, Q – Kt1; 14. B – Kt3, with a win for White.

11.	R – KB1
12. Q – K1	K – R1?

Now Black loses the initiative. The right procedure consisted in 12. .... P – B5 with the deadly threats of P – K6 and P – B6. This loss of a tempo affords White a chance of saving himself.

13. Kt – K2	Q – K2
14. Q – Q1	B – B3
15. Kt – Q4	B – Q2
16. Kt – Kt3	B – K3
17. Kt × B	Q × Kt

Black's most dangerous Bishop has been exchanged off and one can already speak of an advantage for White. But now in fact Lilienthal allows himself to commit an inaccurate move, and the highly interesting game reaches a friendly outcome.

    18. R – Q6?

Correct was *18.* Q – R1, Q–K2; *19.* B – K5, or R – Q6.

18.	Q × B
19. R × B	K – R2
20. P– KR3	R – B1
21. B – Kt3	Q – K6
22. B – B2	Q – B7
23. B – Kt3	R – B6
24. R – K8	R – Q6
25. Q – R5	Q – K8 ch

Drawn by perpetual check on the squares KKt6 and K8.

V. THE DYNAMIC CENTRE

Let us now pass over to the last of the various types of pawn centre which are considered here, namely, the dynamic centre. This could also be termed the unclear centre. 'Pawn formations in a dynamic centre' is a phrase which we use to describe positions in which the fate of the centre pawns is not settled. Perhaps they may chance to disappear from the board, or they may stand watching each other, or perhaps they may succeed in forming a closed centre. Perhaps either player may obtain a mobile or a fixed centre. It is in effect not clear what will happen in the centre.

Pawn formations in a dynamic centre can transpose into any one of the types of position we have already discussed.

The player's attention must be concentrated on the centre. The strategic aim is to obtain a satisfactory stabilization of the centre or else to force one's opponent into a pawn formation that he does not want to have. Sometimes it happens that neither side can wait for the stabilization of the pawn position before being forced to set in motion a flank attack. But it is in just such a case that one must be on the look-out for the enemy counter-thrust in the centre. When such an attack is set in motion at the right time it can annihilate all plans of attack on the wing.

An example of the method of play in such positions can be studied in the game Smyslov–Kotov (Moscow Championship, 1943).

Kotov

69

Smyslov

The position in the centre is unclear. Black has two ways of exchanging off the White pawn on K4, by P – KB4 or by P – Q4. White deems the first threat to be the most dangerous and renders it impracticable.

1.	P – KKt4	QR – Q1

Black turns his attention to the other possibility of breaking open the centre – by P – Q4.

2.	K – R1	Kt – K3
3.	B – Q2	P – Q4

Now he has achieved his purpose. White cannot exchange on Q4 as then Black would control the Q5 square and the central lines, thereby obtaining an ideal position.

4.	Kt – B3	P – Q5?

A strategic mistake of a kind that is here the equivalent of a grave oversight. Black should have tried to open up the centre since an exchange of the K Bishop and the thrust P – KKt4 would have implied a serious weakening of White's King's position. Black should have played *4. . . . . P × P !*, after which White's position would have had a brittle, fragile appearance, both after 5. P × P, Kt – Q5; 6. QR – Q1, Q – B3 and after 5. Kt × P, Q – B3; 6. Q – R3, P – B4; 7. P × P, R × P, above all having consideration for the King's vulnerable position. Instead, by closing the centre, Black shows that White's earlier play was fully justified. Now Smyslov's King-side attack plays itself.

| 5. Kt – K2 | Kt – B3 |

Black should still have made an attempt to open up the centre by 5. .... P – B5; 6. P × P, P – Q6.

6. Q – R3	K – R2
7. Kt – Kt3	P – B3
8. Kt – B5!	

A remarkable sacrifice that in fact Black should not have accepted.

8.	P × Kt
9. KtP × P	Kt – B2
10. R – KKt1	Kt – K1
11. R – Kt6	

And White soon won.

This served as a very good example of a game in which the centre was undefined. We shall now examine two further positions in which the struggle concerns a favourable pawn formation in the centre.

Smyslov

Geller

VARIOUS PAWN POSITIONS IN THE CENTRE

This position occurred in the game Geller–Smyslov in the Candidates' Tournament, 1953, at Zurich. The struggle in the centre is in full swing. What sort of pawn position will eventually be produced and will it be to White's or to Black's advantage? Experience has shown that White gets the advantage when he can establish his centre pawns on the squares QB3, QB4, Q4, K4, KB5, and when, at the same time, the Black pawns are placed on QB4, Q3, K3, and KB2. In the event of Black, on his side, being able to arrive at a pawn formation on QB4, Q3, K3, KB4, while the White pawns are on QB3, QB4, Q4, K4 and KB4, then he obtains a position that is easily defensible.

The moves that immediately follow are characterized by both players striving to obtain an advantageous pawn position.

1. P – K4   Kt – K1

He prepares to meet White's P – B4 with the counter-thrust of P – B4 himself.

2. Q – R4

Here the Queen does nothing. More energetic was *2.* P –B4, P – B4; *3.* Kt – Kt3.

2. . . . .   Q – B1 !

An important post for the Queen in the fight for the centre. From this point it defends both the QR3 and QB3 squares, indirectly attacks the pawn on QB5, and parries the threat of P × P by an eventual Kt – K4.

3. B – K3   P – Q3
4. QR – Q1   Kt – R4
5. P × P

White chooses an incorrect solution of the centre problem. Correct was *5.* P – Q5! This move would have led to a position in which anything might have happened, whereas now the initiative gradually passes into Black's hands.

5. . . . .   QP × P
6. P – K5   Q – B3
7. Q – B2

Exchange of Queens does not of course come into question since then White would lose his pawn on QB4.

7.	. . . .	P – B4
8.	Q – R2	Q – R5
9.	Kt – B4	Kt – B2
10.	B – B2	Q – K1
11.	B – Kt3	P – KKt4

Matters in the centre have developed to Black's advantage. The White pawn on K5 is weak, as are those on QB3 and QB4, and Black has the opportunity of occupying the only open line. Smyslov drives away the Knight from its strong post on KB4 with his KtP.

12.	Kt – R3	P – R3
13.	P – B3	Q – K2
14.	Kt – B2	QR – Q1
15.	Kt – Q3	Q – Kt2
16.	P – B4	R – Q2
17.	Kt – B1	KR – Q1
18.	R × R	R × R

Black now has definitive possession of the open file. Geller's ensuing attempt to obtain vigorous play is easily beaten back by the excellently developed Black pieces.

19.	Q – K2	Kt – Q4
20.	B – Q2	Kt × KBP
21.	B × Kt	P × B
22.	R × P	Q – Kt4
23.	P – Kt3	K – R2
24.	K – B2	Q – Q1
25.	Q – R5	R – KKt2
26.	Q – K2	R – Q2

Repetition of moves in time trouble.

27.	Q – R5	Q – Kt4
28.	Q – K8	Q – K2
29.	Q × Q ch	R × Q
30.	B – R2	R – Q2

The exchange of Queens has given Black the opportunity of

utilizing the open lines without having to fear any counter-attack against his King, which is rather precariously placed. Now, by exact play, Smyslov makes his advantage tell.

31.	K – K2	B – Kt2
32.	B – Kt1	K – Kt1
33.	P – Kt4	P × P
34.	R × P ch	R – Kt2
35.	R – R4	R – Kt8
36.	K – Q2	K – Kt2
37.	B – Q3	B – B6
38.	R – B4	B – R4
39.	Kt – K2	

This accelerates the loss. The energetic move *39. R – B6* would have offered more chances.

39.	....	R – Kt7
40.	K – K3	R – Kt4
41.	P – KR4	R × P ch
42.	K – Q2	Kt – Kt6 ch
43.	K – Q1	R – K6
44.	K – B2	P – K4
45.	R – B2	P – K5

Here White lost by exceeding the time limit. His position was hopeless in any case.

We will now give an example of the unclear centre from the same tournament. It is from the game Boleslavsky–Keres.

Keres

71

Boleslavsky

This position is well known in text-books on opening theory. In the ensuing moves both sides usually contend for the best pawn formation in the centre. In practice these two continuations occur – exchange on K5 and the advance P – Q5. Often we get a position with an open centre that is followed by a general exchange of pawns. For the present game Keres had prepared a new solution of the opening problem.

1.	QKt – Q2	R – Q1
2.	Kt – B1	P – Q4!

A highly complicated position! Now White has many different ways of solving the central problem. One advocated by E. Vasiukov is: *3.* P × KP, P × P; *4.* Kt(B1) – Q2, P × Kt; *5.* P × Kt, B × BP; *6.* Q × P, B – K3; *7.* Kt – K4, B – K2; *8.* Q – R5. Boleslavsky decides to liquidate all the centre pawns and transpose play to a position with an open centre. This is, as we shall see, a bad solution.

3.	KP × P	KP × P
4.	P × P	Kt × P
5.	Q – K2	B – Kt2
6.	Kt – Kt3	P × P
7.	Kt × P	

The pawns have vanished from the centre – the centre is open. In the play with the pieces that now occurs Black quickly seizes the initiative.

7.	....	P – Kt3
8.	B – R6	B – KB3
9.	Kt – Kt3	Kt – QB5
10.	Kt – K4	B × P
11.	Kt(Kt3) – B5	

Boleslavsky offers an exchange sacrifice. After *11.* QR – Kt1, or *11.* QR – Q1, White would have, in any case, been unable to withstand the pressure of the Black pieces on the Queen's wing.

11.	....	B × R
12.	R × B	P – B4

13. Kt × B	Q × Kt
14. Kt – B5	Q – B3
15. Kt – Q3	Kt – B6
16. Q – K1	Q – B3
17. P – B4	Kt – K5

White might have spared himself further exertion and resigned the game here.

18. K – R2	Q – B6
19. Q – QKt1	Kt(B5) – Q7
20. Q – QB1	R × Kt
21. B × R	Q × B
22. Q – B7	Kt – B6 ch
resigns.	

Let us summarize. In positions with a dynamic centre, play should be concentrated on building up as advantageous a centre as possible. It is obvious that an undefined centre can transpose to any one of the four categories we have discussed earlier.

We have now considered the problems concerning pawn formations in the centre. Chess-masters always pay heed to the particular topography in the middle of the board and force their opponent to adopt one type of play or other in accordance with the characteristics of the terrain.

The player who wants to learn how to play chess properly must make himself thoroughly conversant with all the kinds of pawn groupings that may arise in the centre and handle them in play as correctly as possible.

5

THE ART OF ANALYSIS

P. Keres

Every chess-player who at some time or another has played in a serious tournament is acquainted with the agony that accompanies an adjourned game.* No matter whether a game is adjourned in a good, bad, or even position, it always has a discouraging effect on a player's humour. An unclear adjourned position can even destroy his sleep and his appetite: he continues to see before his eyes the Rooks, Knights, and pawns. And when the adjourned position is bad the player's outlook and temper are affected, this in turn harmfully affecting his play again later on in the tournament. An adjourned position must be submitted to a thorough analysis and this sometimes consumes not only an evening but often many days. Moreover, it may happen that despite long analysis one is still unable to come to a clear conclusion and hence one does not rightly know how one should best proceed. In such cases one usually decides upon the continuation that offers the best practical chances. Obviously one must take into consideration in these cases which of the possible variations pose the opponent the greatest problems both from the psychological and technical playing points of view and how one can thereby increase the practical chances. Finally, one must also reckon with the fact that there may arise, both in one's own and in one's opponent's analysis, errors that conduce to surprises for both sides.

It does not lie within the scope of this book to take up the question as to whether it is right to charge tournament players with the burden of adjourned games. However, so long as it happens that in most tournaments games are adjourned after five hours' play, to be resumed the next day or still later, then one must take this additional burden into consideration. The

* In competitive chess games are usually adjourned if unfinished after five hours' play, and resumed at a later stage in the competition. (Ed.)

172

debates that take place once every ten years or so concerning the abolition of adjourned games stem chiefly from Capablanca who indicated one way of solving the problem. The time of play should be arranged to start somewhat earlier and, after a short pause for a meal, the games should be continued without the players being granted permission to analyse in the meantime.

However this may be, we are not yet so far advanced that adjourned games have disappeared from the scene and we must therefore concern ourselves with them whether we like it or not. One thing is clear – the adjourned game exacts great trouble and labour from the player. How one divides up this labour and what methods one employs in dealing with it are naturally very much a matter of individual taste. One man likes to glance at the position immediately after the game 'has been adjourned; another defers this till he has had a peaceful sleep and will concentrate on it only after day has dawned. In my opinion there is no general rule concerning this, and therefore each player must choose the method that suits best his character and customary method of working.

Since none of my colleagues has written about and described his methods I must in the following pages concern myself with the many years' experience I have had in this respect. But I should point out that it has not been my intention to elaborate any complete system for analysing adjourned games. The following examples merely stem from my experiences and are designed to present a picture of the work involved.

Even the reader who never frequents the playing arena and has no intention whatsoever of participating in tournaments will, I think, derive some entertainment from the following analyses. For, over the board as well, one always has to work out sequences of moves and search for ideas, even though one cannot go so deeply into the matter as one can in analysing an adjourned position.

For beginners, insight into an expert's way of thinking may perhaps, too, spur them on to a more knowledgeable striving after tactical finesses which would bear fruit in the shape of strategical ideas in their own play.

I begin the practical examples with the game Szapiel–Keres,

played in the international tournament at Szczawno–Zdrój (Bad Salzbrunn), 1950. The game was adjourned after Black's fortieth move (*40. . . . . P – R6*) in the following position, and this gave both players sufficient time to make themselves thoroughly familiar with the finesses in the position.

Keres

72

Szapiel

The very first glance indicates that Black has a considerable advantage. Although material in the position is equal, Black's passed pawn is a powerful threatening factor that sets White an almost impossible problem to solve. Quite simply, there is threatened a pawn advance of a decisive nature, e.g. *41. R – QR8, P – R7; 42. Kt – K5, Kt – Kt5;* followed by *43. . . . . R – QKt8*, etc. This circumstance meant that I went serenely to bed in an optimistic frame of mind with the foreknowledge that this time the adjourned position would not cost me so much trouble.

However, one cannot treat an adjourned game in so simple a fashion no matter how clear the result may appear to be. Therefore the next day I sat myself down once again at the chess-board to complete my analysis. What showed up on that occasion in a position apparently so simple and how much trouble it was to cost me the reader will soon learn from the ensuing lines.

Let us now study the position in the diagram somewhat more closely. We have already referred to Black's threat, and a cursory analysis has convinced us that there is no direct defence to this threat. White's Knight cannot get back in sufficient time to frustrate Black's winning manoeuvre. So now we must try to see if White has at his disposal adequate attacking possibilities to defeat his opponent's plans. First let us devote attention to the possibility of P – R4 – R5, which creates a mating threat on KR8. Carrying out this plan at once, however, does not lead to the desired goal since after *41.* P – R4, P – R7; *42.* P – R5, there follows *42.* .... R – R8 ch; *43.* K × R, P – R8 = Q ch; and after *44.* K – R2, P – Kt3 all dreams of mating are over and Black wins easily.

But it does not take much time to convince oneself that White's attack can be considerably strengthened. After *41.* P – R4, P – R7, White can first post his Rook better by *42.* R – R8! and after *42.* .... Kt – Kt5 he can again set up his mating threat by *43.* P – R5. Thereafter Black's winning line is indeed not so simple, but at all events it does not necessitate particularly deep analysis. Black in fact plays *43.* .... P –Kt4! and if then *44.* P × P e.p. ch, White's success is at an end after *44.* .... K × P; *45.* Kt – K5 ch, K – B4; *46.* P – B3, R – KB8, and he must give up a Rook. An attempt to complicate this by *44.* R – R7 is also insufficient as Black replies quite simply *44.* .... R – QB8! and his King escapes from the checks, e.g. *45.* Kt × P db ch, K – Kt1; *46.* R – R8 ch, K – Kt2; *47.* R – R7 ch, K – B1; *48.* Kt × P ch, K – K1, or else *45.* Kt – K5 dis ch, K – Kt1; *46.* R – R8 ch, K – Kt2; *47.* R – R7 ch, K – B1; and in both cases the King escapes to the Queen's side.

Thus the first attempt to save the game has failed, but we still have not investigated all the opponent's resources. Further research into the position soon shows that White can win an important tempo with which to counter Black's passed pawn by *41.* R – R8 ch, K – Kt3; *42.* Kt – K5 ch. This defence does not appear to be particularly effective, since with it White surrenders his best trump card – the mating threat. In addition Black's King threatens a decisive penetration via KB4 and

K5. But despite this, the requisite adjournment analysis had to be checked with the utmost accuracy and the greatest care.

And here already the first difficulties emerge. Surprisingly enough, it appears that White can even in this position pose some dangerous threats to the enemy King, and soon one gains the conviction that there can be no talk of an easy winning line. The question is to where the Black King can escape and it is with this problem that we shall concern ourselves more exhaustively in what follows.

Since the ensuing investigations lead to very complicated positions and comprise many variations it is in consequence appropriate to our objective to analyse every possible King move and set out the variations in tabular form. In this way, at any rate, the possible chances of confusion are limited and not particularly harmful.

Keres

73

Szapiel
(Analysis)

Variation A

42. .....   K – R4

It would be all very nice to shield the King from further checks and then to advance with the QR pawn, e.g. *43.* R – R8, P – R7; *44.* Kt – B6, R – QB8; or *44.* Kt – Q3, R – Q8 when

Black wins a piece. But this plan has one snag: the unfavourable position of the Black King.

> **43. R – KKt8!**

This is the saving move! By means of the threat of *44.* R × P, White suddenly obtains a dangerous mating attack.

| *43. ....* | P – R7 |

This line can lead only to a loss. Black has nothing better at his disposal than *43. ....* R – KB8; *44.* R – QR8!, R × P; *45.* R × P, with an approximately equal position.

44. R × P	R – R8 ch
45. K × R	P – R8 = Qch
46. K – R2!	

Now we suddenly perceive that there is no longer any defence against the threat of *47.* P – Kt4 ch, followed by *48.* Kt – B3 mate. After *46. ....* Q – R6; *47.* Kt – B3! Q – Q3 ch; *48.* K – Kt1, the mate on Kt4 cannot be parried.

Thus it did not take me long to reject the move *42. ....* K – R4, so as to concern myself with better possibilities. Next to be considered was *42. ....* K – Kt4.

Variation B (see Diagram 73)

| *42. ....* | K – Kt4 |

This King move looks at first to be better, since now no direct mating lines are threatened against the Black potentate, and also, here as in the preceding variation, the attempt to win by *43.* R – R7 is inadequate. After further investigation, however, I also found in this position some most disagreeable variations that made the win problematic.

> **43. R – KB8!**

With this, Black's King is once again most unpleasantly disturbed. If for example Black follows out his plan logically with *43. ....* P – R7, then there awaits him a disagreeable surprise:

44. P – B4 ch! Kt × P; *45.* P – R4 ch, K × P (after *45.* . . . .
K – R4; *46.* R × Kt, R – R8 ch; *47.* K × R, P – R8 = Q ch;
48. K – R2, with the threat of *49.* P – Kt4 ch, followed by
mate, Black no longer has any winning prospects); *46.* R × Kt
ch, K – Kt4; *47.* R – B2, R – R8 ch (*48.* K – Kt3 was threatened); *48.* K × R, P – R8 = Q ch; *49.* K – R2, and White
retains an easy draw.

Perhaps this move provides an adequate defensive line? But
I could not dismiss the possibilities of *42.* . . . . K – Kt4 so
lightly. After some further exploration I discovered the reply
43. . . . . Kt – B3, and I was already inclined to regard White's
position as hopeless.

43. . . . .   Kt – B3 !

In fact, matters look very gloomy for White, since the Black
King threatens a decisive penetration through B4 and K5;
e.g. *44.* R – B7, K – B4; *45.* R × P, K – K5, and Black must
win by eventually playing his Knight back to the Queen's
wing.

Despite this, I was not altogether satisfied, since playing the
Knight back does not seem very logical and I was far from being
convinced that, among all the possibilities, there might not exist
a continuation that would ensure White adequate counter-play.
Once again I devoted myself to a thorough investigation of the
position and soon I found a strong continuation.

44. R – QR8 !

With this White threatens after, for example, *44.* . . . . P – R4
to win the QRP by *45.* Kt – B4, P – R7; *46.* Kt – K3, followed
by *47.* Kt – B2, and *48.* R × P. This threat cannot be parried by
either of the King moves to B5 or B4. So Black has no choice,
if he does not want to repeat moves by *44.* . . . . Kt – Q4; *45.*
R – KB8.

44. . . . .   P – R7
45. P – B3 !

Now there has arisen a position over which we must pause, as
it contains many interesting possible lines.

Keres

Szapiel
(Analysis)

In theory the position should be won without great difficulty
for Black. All he needs to do is to get his King into active play
via K6; or else, also, he can shield his King's position against
enemy assault and then win by the manoeuvre Kt – B3 – Q4 –
Kt5, followed by R – QKt8. Thus the plan is, taken by itself,
particularly simple, but when we try to put it into practical
working order then we unexpectedly run into great difficulties.
Thus, for instance, the attempt to bring the King across by
45. .... K – B5 would lead at once to the loss of the QRP on
account of 46. Kt – Q3 ch, K – K6; 47. Kt – Kt4. So we must
tackle matters much more carefully. Since for the moment Black
is not directly threatened, there comes into consideration first of
all:

> 45. ....   P – R4

This threatens 46. .... P – R5, when White's King-side
pawns would be lamed. Other attempts would merely have
resulted in a change for the worse. On 45. .... K – B4; there
would ensue 46. R – R5, Kt – Q4; 47. P – Kt3, and Black's
King is once again surrounded by enemies, and also 45. ....
Kt – Q4; 46. P – Kt3, P – R4; 47. P – R4 ch, K – B4; 48.
R – R7, would have led to a similar position, in which Black has
in practice no longer any winning prospects.

However, in reply to the text-move White possesses a surprising riposte.

46. P – R4 ch!   K – B4

There is an interesting variation here: *46. ....* K × P; *47.* R – R5!, K – Kt4 (the continuation *47. ....* Kt – Q4? even leads to a loss on account of *48.* P – B4!, Kt × P; *49.* Kt – B3 ch, K – Kt5; *50.* R – Kt5 mate!); *48.* Kt – Q3 dis ch, Kt – Q4; *49.* Kt – Kt4, and White wins the QRP, whereupon Black's practical winning chances are highly problematical.

47. R – R5   Kt – Q4
48. P – Kt3!

Now Black's pieces are once more so badly placed that his winning chances are reduced to nil. He could try *48. ....* P – KKt4; but then follows *49.* P – Kt4 ch!, P × P (or *49. ....* K – B3; *50.* P × RP, P × P; *51.* P – R6 etc.), *50.* P × P ch, K – B5 (or B3); *51.* P – R5! and White's passed pawn is also a powerful factor in the game.

The variations given above show clearly enough that the attempt to win by *42. ....* K – Kt4 has not got great prospects of success. With this analysis I became convinced more and more every minute that I had fundamentally overestimated my chances in the adjourned position. All the same I was very optimistic indeed as I still had left two logical continuations in *42. ....* K – B4 and *42. ....* K – B3. So down I set myself to work once again.

Variation C (see Diagram 73)

42. ....   K – B4

This King move, in comparison with *42. ....* K – Kt4, wins a valuable tempo as now Black threatens to penetrate decisively with his King via the square K5. Thus Black would win easily after, for example, *43.* R – R8, K – K5; *44.* Kt – B4, P – R7; *45.* Kt – Q2 ch, K – Q6; *46.* Kt – Kt3, R – QKt8; *47.* Kt – B5 ch, K × P; *48.* Kt × P ch, K – K4; etc. Also the continuation *43.* Kt – Q3 (or Q7), would be insufficient on account of

43. .... Kt – B2! but not *43.* .... K – K5; *44.* Kt – B5 ch, etc. White therefore does not have much choice.

43. P – B3	K – B5

Apparently, everything is now in perfect order, since Black's King has evaded the unpleasant mating threat and threatens to encroach on enemy territory via the K6 square. But it became clear that White also, in this seemingly hopeless plight, possessed defensive possibilities that rendered the win highly problematical. Therefore I searched for other possibilities that would perhaps furnish better results. In my search I found nothing better than *43.* .... P – R7, to which White's reply is obviously *44.* R – R8.

Now Black, by *44.* .... K – B5; *45.* R – R3, or *44.* .... P – R4; *45.* P – R4, arrives at positions that I had studied in the analyses of the variations arising out of *43.* .... K – B5, which are mentioned in our analysis below. Naturally, *44.* .... Kt – Kt5? would be absolutely wrong since then *45.* R – B8 ch, K – Kt4; *46.* P – B4 ch, even results in mate. Thus there only remains *44.* .... K – B3 so as to attempt to escape eventually with the King to the Queen's side.

It hardly needs any exhaustive analysis to establish the inadequacy of this idea. White plays *45.* R – R7, and threatens to weave a mating net by *46.* P – R4, so that *45.* .... K – Kt4 is, practically speaking, forced. Now Black seeks to get his King into safety via B5 or R3, but White continues to possess a large number of defensive possibilities. To name only a few, one has to reckon with: *46.* P – Kt3, P – R4; *47.* R × P ch, K – R3; *48.* R – R7, Kt – Kt5 (after *48.* .... P – R5; *49.* P × P, and only now *49.* .... Kt – Kt5, White saves the game by *50.* Kt – Kt4 ch, followed by *51.* Kt – K5 ch, etc.); *49.* P – R4, R – QB8; *50.* P – Kt4, P × P; *51.* P × P, and Black has no time for *51.* .... P – R8 = Q, since mate is threatened by *52.* P – Kt4 ch, etc.

So the line *43.* .... P – R7 proved to be in no way a strengthening of Black's method of play, and hence I had to retain the move *43.* .... K – B5. Since this position is also of importance for later analyses we show it in the diagram.

Keres

75

Szapiel
(Analysis)

44. R – R8!

This Rook move, which prevents *44. .... K – K6;* on account of *45. R × P ch,* followed by *46. Kt – B4 ch,* undoubtedly sets Black the most difficult problems. The other possibility *44. Kt – B4, P – R7; 45. R – B8 ch, Kt – B3* (somewhat simpler is perhaps *45. .... K – Kt4); 46. R – QR8,* leads after *46. .... R – QB8!* to the win of the Knight, but only after many complications. The continuation might be: *47. P – Kt3 ch, K – Kt4* (also *47. ... K × P; 48. Kt – K5 ch, K – K5; 49. R × P, K × P,* yields good winning chances); *48. P – B4 ch, K – R4; 49. R – R5 ch* (or *49. P – Kt4 ch, K – R5; 50. Kt – K3, Kt × P ch,* followed by *51. .... P – R8 = Q,* etc.), *49. .... P – Kt4; 50. P – Kt4 ch, K – R5; 51. Kt – K3, Kt × P ch;* followed by *52. .... P – R8 = Q* and Black wins.

44. ....   P – R7

For the moment I could find no other way of making any progress. Now there is threatened once more *45. .... K – K6.*

45. R – R3   Kt – B6

Black's attack can get no further. Pawn moves such as *45. .... P – Kt3; 46. P – Kt3 ch, K – B4; 47. P – Kt4 ch,*

K – B3; *48.* R – R7, or *45.* .... P – R4; *46.* P – R4, P – Kt4; *47.* P – Kt3 ch, K – B4; *48.* P – Kt4 ch, P × P (or also *48.* .... K – B3; *49.* P × RP, P × P; *50.* P – R6, etc.); *49.* P × P ch, K – K5; *50.* P – R5, give Black absolutely no hope of winning. In addition to the text-move *45.* .... Kt – K6 also came into consideration. Thereupon White can hold the game in two ways: in the first place, quite simply by *46.* Kt – Q3 ch, K – Kt4; *47.* Kt – Kt4, etc., and in the second, very prettily by *46.* P – Kt3 ch!, K – B4; *47.* R – R7, since now Black must not play *47.* .... Kt – B8 ch; *48.* K – Kt2, Kt × P; *49.* K × Kt!, R – Kt8 ch; *50.* K – R4, and White wins, since mate is threatened on KB7.

46. P – Kt3 ch!	K – K6

Or *46.* .... K – B4; *47.* R – R7! With more mating threats.

47. R × Kt ch	K × P
48. R – R3	K × Kt

In the Rook ending that has been reached Black has, it is true, a pawn more, but the Rook's passive position makes it more than doubtful if it is possible to utilize the pawn plus for real winning chances. From the analytical standpoint, however, the position is not satisfactory, and so, with a heavy heart, I had to lay on one side the continuation *42.* .... K – B4. Everything now hung on the question as to whether there was anything in the last possibility – *42.* .... K – B3.

Variation D (see Diagram 73)

42.	K – B3

This move had not at first glance appealed to me since I wanted either to escape from checks with the King or else to enable it to penetrate as swiftly as possible via K5 or K6. Now that these attempts had failed the move at once seemed to me more promising. Why indeed should Black allow his King to wander around in the midst of various mating nets when he obviously could, tranquilly and peacefully, play it to the Queen's wing? It is true that in the meantime White obtains a

number of disagreeable checking threats, but that is perhaps
not so dangerous when there are only two attacking White
pieces? At all events, I now had to investigate this possibility
more closely.

> *43.* R – R8 !

Undoubtedly the best defence. Now, in order to prevent *44.*
R – R7, when Black's King is again cut off, and the previously
analysed possibilities would be repeated, Black must at once
allow his King to begin a long march.

> *43.* ....   K – K2
> *44.* R – R7 ch   K – Q1

Keres

76

Szapiel
(Analysis)

This seemed more or less forced here. I looked once again
with confidence to the future, as in reality my opponent had no
chances of making a draw by perpetual check. The lines *45.*
R – R8 ch, K – B2; or *45.* Kt – B6 ch, K – K1 lead to nothing
and White also reaps a lean harvest after *45.* Kt – B7 ch, K –
B1; *46.* Kt – Q6 ch, K – Kt1; *47.* R – Kt7 ch, K – R1. Could
this really be the solution of the problem? Before coming to
such a conclusion, however, other defensive possibilities had to
be taken into account. Black does in fact require still more time
for the promotion of his QRP to Queen.

And scarcely had such a thought crossed my mind than the refutation also revealed itself.

45. R × KtP!

White utilizes the time at his disposal to demolish an enemy pawn and to obtain chances of bringing about a drawn ending by sacrificing a Knight for the QRP. Now Black is faced with the problem of how to get any further with his QRP, since nothing can be done except by this method.

45. ....   P – R7

Should Black try to bring his Knight to help the pawn on, then he merely opens up fresh defensive possibilities in so doing. After 45. .... Kt – Kt5 there would, in fact, follow 46. R – Kt7! and now both 46. .... P – R7; 47. R × Kt, R – R8 ch; 48. K × R, P – R8 = Q ch; 49. K – R2, and 46. .... R – QKt8; 47. R × Kt!, P – R7; 48. R – R4, P – R8 = Q; 49. R × Q, R × R; 50. Kt – B7 ch, followed by 51. Kt × P, result in an ending that White can no longer lose.

If Black tries to prepare the move Kt – Kt5 by 45. ... K – B1 so as to meet 46. Kt – B6 with 46. .... R – QB8, then White plays 46. R – QR7! Then if 46. .... Kt – Kt5, White can, among other possibilities, force a drawn ending by 47. R – R4, P – R7; 48. R × Kt.

46. Kt – B6 ch!

More exact than an immediate 46. R – QR7, since this deprives Black's Knight of the QKt5 square. Black's King cannot go to B1 since after 47. Kt – R7 ch, it must eventually be played to K1.

46. ....   K – K1
47. R – QR7   K – B1

At once 47. .... R – QB8 will not do on account of 48. R – R8 ch, followed by 49. Kt – K5 ch, and 50. R × P. After 47. .... Kt – B6, however, there can follow 48. Kt – Kt4, R – QKt8; 49. Kt × P, R – R8; 50. R – R6! and Black must either allow 51. Kt – Kt4, or else give up both his last pawns.

THE ART OF THE MIDDLE GAME

The text-move serves the purpose of preparing the threat of
48. . . . . R – QB8.

| *48*. | R – R8 ch | K – Kt2 |
| *49*. | R – R7 ch | |

With this Black once more finds himself at the beginning of
his task. For if, in fact, his King were to go to the third rank,
there would then follow *50*. Kt – K5 (with or without check)!,
and again we have a position known to us from the analysis in
Variation C. The difference lies only in the fact that Black has
sacrificed the KKtP and that is far from being an advantage.

So, too, Variation D had also gone with the wind and I sat
there as wise as when I had begun the analysis. Was in truth all
my trouble in vain and could not the position be won at all? As
all chess-masters surely know from their own practice, it is not
at all unusual that one takes a very optimistic view of the
position at the adjournment of the game, only to become convinced by analysis later on that there is really not so much in the
position after all. Hence one should not allow oneself to be
contented with the result of one single analysis, but one should,
on some occasions repeatedly, try to penetrate more deeply
into the secrets of the position. This is what I did here. I had
not found anything in the first 'round', and, since I had sufficient time before the game was due to be resumed, I left the
whole matter till the opportunity should arise the next day of
examining it once again in the most thorough manner possible.
The fact that one is already familiar with the finesses of the
position allows one to examine it on a subsequent occasion
with considerably less expenditure of energy.

Naturally, in checking one's analysis one must in the first place
try to find the mistake or inexactitude that may have led to a
faulty judgement. And if this essay should, in spite of everything, fail to yield a satisfactory result, then one must endeavour
to find the variation that contains the most opportunities for
one's opponent to make a mistake and which thereby comprises
the best practical winning chances. So, the next immediate task
is to find improvements in the analysis!

With regard to Variations A and B with *42*. . . . . K – R4 and

42. .... K – Kt4 I soon abandoned my efforts as I found in fact that there was nothing fresh to discover. Nor in Variation D with *42. .... K – B3* could I find any strengthening of Black's method of play. I therefore concentrated all my attention on Variation C and commenced my researches after the moves *42. .... K – B4; 43. P – B3, K – B5.*

After studying the position for a long time I found some little hope in the idea of answering *44. R – R8, P – R7; 45. R – R3,* with *45. .... K – Kt4.* With this Black threatens, for example, after *46. P – Kt3,* to obtain a niche for his King on R3 by *46. .... P – R4* and thereby to evade the continual mating threats. I had at first discarded this move on account of *46. P – R4 ch,* since *46. .... K × P; 47. P – B4, Kt × P; 48. P – Kt3 ch,* would have led to the loss of the Knight. A further check-up, however, showed that instead of *47. .... Kt × P?* Black has a stronger continuation in *47. .... Kt – B6!* Now there is threatened *48. .... R – QB8* followed by *49. .... P – R8 = Q,* and after *48. R × Kt, R – R8 ch; 49. K × R, P – R8 = Q ch* the Rook is lost.

At last a winning chance had been discovered, but this was still not altogether satisfactory, since White had many other defensive possibilities. Thus for example White could try *46. R – R8,* after *45. .... K – Kt4;* so as to obtain, in the event of *46. .... P – R4,* a clearly drawn position by *47. P – R4 ch!, K – B5* (neither *47. .... K × P; 48. P – B4,* nor *47. .... K – B3; 48. R – R7,* yield anything for Black); *48. R – R3.* No clear result is to be obtained from the try *46. .... Kt – Kt5; 47. P – R4 ch, K × P* (after *47. .... K – B3; 48. R – R7,* or *47. .... K – B5; 48. Kt – Kt4,* unpleasant mating threats emerge); *49. Kt – Kt4,* since White threatens Kt – Kt4 – K3 – B2 etc.

The best prospects for Black are afforded by the continuation *46. .... Kt – B6,* since then *47. P – R4 ch, K × P; 48. R – R5,* can be met by *48. .... K – Kt4!* True, White could also put up a stiff resistance here by *49. Kt – Q3 dis ch, K – B3; 50. Kt – Kt4, R – QKt8; 51. Kt × P, R – R8; 52. R – R3, Kt × Kt; 53. R – R7,* but Black would none the less have a whole piece more. But *47. P – Kt3!* causes Black fresh difficulties. After

47. .... R – K8; 48. P – R4 ch, K – R4; *49.* R – R5!, mate in two is suddenly threatened, and hence Black has scarcely anything better than *48. ....* K – B3; *49.* R – R7, R × Kt; *50.* P × R ch, K × P. One cannot say at first glance that this end game is one hundred per cent won.

As we have seen, the winning variations with *45. ....* K – Kt4 were not altogether beyond dispute, but at all events I now had something that could be tried in practicable play. I was not, however, satisfied with it and therefore decided to search still further, setting aside the variation to serve as a promising reserve solution. I had the feeling that there must exist a main solution that could make Black's advantage concrete in absolutely clear fashion. So, refusing to weary of the search, I continued my investigations.

I was convinced that the solution of the problem must lie in Variation C, and therefore I devoted my attention chiefly to the position in the diagram.

Keres

77

Szapiel
(Analysis)

The pawn advance, *44. ....* P – R7, as analysed above, proved unsuccessful, but what else could Black try? The King could not well go to K6 on account of *45.* R × P; a pawn action on the King's wing would be meaningless; and so Knight moves to either Kt5 or B6 White could reply with the very good *45.* P – R4, since the Black King can never step on the square K6.

In this seemingly crystal-clear situation I suddenly hit upon a paradoxical thought that would never have come to anybody at first glance, namely, the sacrifice of the one pride and joy of the Black position, the pawn on R6.

44. ....   K – K6!!

It is well-nigh incredible that the way to win lies in the surrender of the strong passed pawn on R6, but this is in fact the case. One might ask how can Black win if he gives up his passed pawn and at the same time exchanges Rooks, coming down to a Knight ending with a pawn less, and when furthermore all the pawns are on the King's wing. And yet a closer analysis will demonstrate that the solution of the problem in the position lies precisely in this improbable move.

45. R × P ch

Forced, since 45. Kt – B4 ch, K – B7; 46. Kt × P, Kt – K6 would lose at once.

45. ....   R × R
46. Kt – B4 ch   K – B7
47. Kt × R   Kt – K6!

Here is the position that I had foreseen on my forty-fourth move (K – K6) and which I now wanted to analyse more closely. It is easy to see that Black gets back his pawn without any trouble, but this by itself does not mean a win. What particularly attracted me about this position was the fact that the White forces are most unfavourably placed. The King takes no part in the fight, and at least two moves are required for the Knight before it can be brought back into play once again. I was therefore justified in hoping that I would not only win back my pawn but would also make some headway in the position to the extent of rendering and keeping the White King inefficacious. A pawn more in a Knight ending is indeed normally decisive when the rest of the pieces are well placed.

Thus the position was worthy of a closer analysis, and so I started on the different variations.

48. P – B4

After some reflection, I came to the conclusion that this advance, by which White procures for himself a passed pawn on the Q file was his most dangerous counter-chance. The attempt to defend the Kt pawn by 48. P – Kt4, leads after 48. . . . . Kt – B8 ch; 49. K – R1, Kt – Kt6 ch; 50. K – R2, K × P; to a position in which White after 51. Kt – Kt5, Kt – K7 also loses his Q pawn with a hopeless ending as the sequel. Similarly the counter-attack 48. Kt – Kt5, Kt × P; 49. Kt – B7, produces nothing as Black protects his K pawn by 49. . . . . Kt – B5 and then continues with 50. . . . . K × P with an easily won ending.

So White has nothing better than to put his trust in the liberation of the Q pawn, but this counter-chance too proves to be inadequate.

    48. . . . .   Kt × P
    49. P – B5   P × P
    50. P – Q5

This passed pawn would have assured White very good counter-play had his King not been so unfavourably placed and exposed to a mating attack. In the long run Black will win without much difficulty.

    50. . . . .   Kt – B5
    51. P – Q6   P – Kt4

Here I ended my analysis since I regarded Black's position as clearly won. In actual fact, now 52. P – Q7 will not do, as then Black's Kt pawn goes on directly to Queen and deliver mate: 52. . . . . P – Kt5; 53. P × P, P × P; 54. P – Q8 = Q, P – Kt6 ch, etc.

At last I had solved the difficult problem set by the adjourned position and found a way that led to a clearly won position. I was therefore feeling most content when the time came for the game to be resumed. Indeed, the game followed the last analysis exactly. My opponent too had thoroughly investigated the position and thought he had excellent prospects of saving the game, since he had not noticed the surprising continuation 44. . . . . K – K6! When I made this move on the board my opponent at first believed that it was a blunder, peeped in surprised fashion at me, and then took the pawn. Only after *47. .... Kt – K6!* did he once again delve deeply into the position, but naturally could find no saving clause. After *51. .... P – Kt4* he tried *52. Kt – B2, P – Kt5; 53. P × P, P × P; 54. Kt – K1,* so as to obtain a draw after *54. .... K × Kt?* by *55. K – Kt3.* There followed, however, *54. .... P – Kt6 ch; 55. K – R1, K × Kt;* and then White resigned. He must lose yet another tempo by *56. K – Kt1 (56. P – Q7, K – B7),* and then Black has the choice between *56. .... P – R4; 57. P – Q7, Kt – K3,* or the more forcing *56. .... K – K7; 57. P – Q7, K – B6!; 58. P – Q8 = Q, Kt – K7 ch; 59. K – B1, P – Kt7 ch; 60. K – K1, P – Kt8 = Q ch; 61. K – Q2, Q – B8 ch; 62. K – Q3, Q – B6 mate.*

The example described above is but one of many that a tournament player comes across in tournaments. It does happen, too, that the master often is given no pause for the resumption of play between rounds, but must content himself with laying aside the adjourned game in favour of preparations for the next round. That these tasks often demand no less work and concentration than the normal game, the example given above should demonstrate. On this occasion, at any rate, the great work was crowned with success. It often happens, however, that one works at an adjourned position for many days without obtaining a satisfactory result. Hence it is easy to understand that many chess-masters are of the opinion that it would be a blessing if in the future it would not be necessary to adjourn any game.

The example shown above might give rise to the supposition that analysis of adjourned games is merely a question of industrious application. Thus if one had sufficient time one could discover all the secrets of a position at home and the game, on resumption of play, would then proceed automatically in accordance with a settled design. So, given sufficient energy, adjourned games are then no longer any problem!

Such a conception is however basically false. In the case of the game Szapiel–Keres it could perhaps be justified a little, in that there White had only a narrow path of defence and the adjourned position evinced a seemingly forced character. But hundreds of examples are to be found in which the adjourned position reveals such a richness of complicated possibilities that one cannot at all, not even after many days' analysis at home, arrive at their complete clarification. In such cases the decisive factor is usually the player's individual ability to appraise the situation correctly and find a plan of play that promises to give the greatest practical possibility of success, a plan which must subsequently be pursued with great exactitude over the board.

In addition to the great number of variations that merit consideration there is, too, another factor, which sometimes prevents one from fully clarifying one's ideas about the adjourned position. This is the limited amount of time that the player has at his disposal. It may happen that one has to resume play very quickly after the adjournment, or that one has so many adjourned games that it is quite impossible to work them out with sufficient thoroughness. In such cases one must naturally refrain from a more exact study of the variations and instead work out as quickly as possible a good plan that can yield practical chances of success.

That in such cases disagreeable surprises may occur and the actual play fail always to follow the plan designed, is only to be expected. To elucidate this assertion I give as an illustration the following adjourned position from my game against Fairhurst in the Hastings Tournament of 1954–5.

Keres

78

Fairhurst

The game was played in the last round and was of decisive importance for the ranking order in the prize list. Smyslov had already finished play in the tournament and led me by a whole point, but I could still catch up with him if the adjourned game turned out well for me. It was therefore necessary for me to win at all costs. I was, however, so far in advance of my other rivals that they could not come abreast with me even if I lost the game. So I was only interested in a win; both the draw and the loss would have meant I should have gained second prize.

A long series of exchanges had taken place before the adjournment. I harboured the hope of gaining victory through utilizing my good Knight against my opponent's inactive Bishop. I had little time for analysis as the game was due to be resumed after an interval of only two hours. Since however the position was considerably simplified I hoped to be able to extract the most important lines from it despite the shortness of time available. In this time trouble of mine, grandmaster Ragosin, who was also at Hastings, came to my help, and after some pondering over the position we soon hit upon the following idea.

White had sealed the move, and it was not difficult to discover his move, since the pawn attacked on Q4 can only be guarded in one way.

36. B – Kt2

Our labours started with this position as our point of departure. It does not require much thought to realize that White is quite out of danger once he arrives at 37. K – B2. In that event, Black can in no way penetrate with his Knight, nor can he help matters in any way by advancing his King-side pawns. If Black wants to play for a win then only one move comes into question.

36. . . . .   Kt – K6

Now 37. K – B2 is prevented on account of 37. . . . . Kt – Q8 ch. White must nevertheless prepare this move as quickly as possible if he does not want to fight without his King, and the next move is therefore practically speaking, forced.

37. B – B1

But what should Black do now? To return to B4 with his Knight would be the same as to acknowledge himself contented with the draw. And *37. . . . .* Kt – Q8 would entail danger of losing, since then White would suddenly arrive at the powerful threat of B – B7. So there is nothing else but

37.	Kt – B7
38. B – Kt2	

This position must perforce be attained if Black wishes to make an attempt to win from the diagram position. On a closer examination our 'win' makes a most pitiable impression. The Knight is stuck on QB7 and the threat is to capture it by K – Kt1 – B2 – K2 – Q2, since the pawn ending after the exchange of Knight for Bishop on QR6 would be easily won for White.

So the whole variation will not do. We were just about thinking of a return to the original position to see if there was a quiet continuation which contained practical chances, when Ragosin drew my attention to an extraordinary idea.

38.	P – B4
39. K – B2	

The pawn advance P – KB5 is not so easily prevented, as *39.* P – Kt3?, Kt – K8 would cost a pawn on account of the double threat *40. . . . .* Kt × P ch and *40. . . . .* Kt – Q6, and *39.* P – B4 would stalemate White's Bishop. Black could then play his Knight by force to K5 and would have considerably improved his winning prospects on account of White's bad Bishop. If any concrete result would come from all this is another question, but one seldom makes such a move as *39.* P – B4 willingly.

39.	P – B5

With this Black has ensured a retreat via K6 for his Knight and blunted the point of the threat K – B2 – K2 – Q2. White's Bishop is completely and permanently stalemated, and if White continues passively, then Black can press forward with his pawns on the King's wing and thus create real winning chances for himself. So White must undertake something on the King's side.

40. P – Kt4!

Keres

79

Fairhurst
(Analysis)

40. ....   P × P e.p. ch

Again Black is confronted with an awkward choice. If he refrains from this capture and allows White the possibility of *41.* P – R4, then the position is once again closed and the result would be a drawn ending. The text-move has, all the same, a dangerous look about it, since White can in fact renew the old threat of K – B2 – K2 – Q2 after *41.* P × P, and it is not at first glance easy to see how Black can bring help to his Knight. But it is precisely in this variation, seemingly so plausible, that Ragosin's artful idea lies.

41. P × P

A study of the other possibility *41.* K × P, leads one at first to the conviction that Black's prospects are not particularly bright. White once again threatens to capture the Knight by K – B2 – K2 – Q2, and after *41.* .... Kt – K8; *42.* B – B1, White obtains counter-play by means of the threat of B – B4 – B7, or by B – Kt5 – Q8. If, however, Black tries *41.* .... Kt – K6, then the opponent's King penetrates decisively into the centre by *42.* K – B4! after which White has nothing more to fear.

Despite this possibility we decided to keep on looking at the variation, and that with good reason. In the first place Black has in fact no other way of proceeding with any possible hope of winning; in the second place he risks nothing, since after *41.* K × P, he always has a draw in hand by *41.* .... Kt – K8; *42.* B – B1, Kt – B7. And in the third it is not at all obvious that the adversary will play *41.* K × P, as he might entertain thoughts to the effect that the opponent's Knight will let itself be captured after *41.* P × P. This was a practical chance and it had to be taken willy-nilly.

| *41.* .... | P – R4! |

Once again aid is given to the enclosed Knight. White may not now attack it by *42.* K – K2, P – Kt4; *43.* K – Q2, since then Black obtains a dangerous passed pawn by *43.* .... P – R5 and thus thwarts the plans for capturing the Knight. So once again the prospects look rosy for Black, but White's resources are still not exhausted.

| *42.* P – B4! |

With this the Knight's fate is sealed, since against the threat of K – K2 – Q2 × Kt, there is no longer any defence. It was in this position, seemingly so hopeless for Black, that Ragosin demonstrated his interesting idea.

42.	K – B2
43. K – K2	K – B3
44. K – Q2	K – B4

The pawn ending after *44.* .... Kt – R6; *45.* B × Kt, P × B; *46.* K – B2, is won for White, as Black's King cannot proceed against the pawns on White's King's wing on account of the possibility of P – QKt4. With the text-move Black makes his long-planned Knight sacrifice by which, it is true, he obtains only one pawn for the piece, but is able to create a most dangerous passed pawn on the KR file.

| *45.* K × Kt | K – Kt5 |

With this we reach the main point of Ragosin's winning plan. Black now wins the pawn on KKt6 and apparently forces the opponent to give up his Bishop for the KRP, whereupon the pawn ending is easily won for Black. But White still has a poisoned arrow in his quiver, and this must be taken into consideration.

46. B – B3!

Now 47. B × P is threatened, and after 46. .... P × B there follows 47. P – Kt4. Black, however, is in a position to ignore his opponent's threat and to follow out his plans on the King's wing.

46. ....   K × P

Against the threatened advance of the KRP White has clearly nothing better than 47. B × P, which, however, leads to a most favourable, probably won, Queen ending for Black after 47. .... P × B; 48. P – R5, P – R5, etc. We show the final position of our analysis in the diagram.

Keres

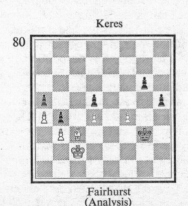

80

Fairhurst
(Analysis)

So we had found something which could at least give practical winning chances. It is true the whole variation is not forced, since we have already observed that the capture 41. K × P, (instead of *41.* P × P) would provide White with adequate counter-play, but all the same I had to try the variation. In other lines White had indeed an easy draw.

Meantime the midday period of rest for lunch was at an end and again I had to hurry back to the tournament hall without being able to check more thoroughly the soundness of our analysis. Most of all, I was interested in the question as to how White would play on his forty-first move if this position should arise.

On the resumption of the game everything proceeded according to plan from the very start. White had made the obvious move *36.* B – Kt2, and we continued comparatively quickly along the lines of our analysis. On the fortieth move I played P × P e.p. ch, and awaited my opponent's reply in a state of considerable tension. To my great surprise Fairhurst captured the pawn by *41.* P × P, without reflection, whereupon of course I played *41.* . . . . P – R4 and, so as to occupy my mind, went and looked at the other adjourned games.

Quietly I walked up and down past the chess-board and naturally anticipated that my opponent would soon play P – B4. But time passed and still Fairhurst had not moved. This astonished me, since in fact White had nothing else than *42.* P – B4. When, all the same, my opponent thought longer and longer I began to interest myself in the position, to discover the reason why he had not played P – B4. So once again I had to check over my adjourned game analysis.

First of all I was able to ascertain whether everything worked all right in the variation *42.* K – K2, P – KKt4, since here White could not in fact capture the Knight without letting Black's KRP proceed to Queen. Then I went on to investigate our main variation and suddenly I came to a rapid halt. I had discerned a huge hole in the analysis that could turn the result upside down! It appeared that White could quietly capture the Knight without falling into a lost Queen ending. On the contrary, he could win the game. Naturally, I no longer felt so contented as I had been a move earlier, and, while my opponent was meditating, I devoted myself to a closer examination of my conclusions. But the result was just as discouraging and now there was nothing left for me to do but to wait and see if my opponent would hit upon the mistake in my analysis or not.

But what had I discovered that was new? We had broken off our investigations at a point where we accepted that White had nothing better than to come down to a Queen ending by 47. B × P. Now, however, to my horror, I discovered the move

47. B – K1 ch!

What in fact does this check do? There seems no great difference if, in the ensuing Queen ending, the Black King stands on either Kt3 or Kt4. But there is a difference! The whole point lies in the fact that White, after 47. ... K – Kt5, is not at all forced to sacrifice his Bishop on Kt4 but can continue quite simply with 48. K – Q3. After 48. .... P – R5; 49. K – K3, P – R6; 50. K – B2, White reaches the KRP with his King in the nick of time and then wins easily by means of the threat of 49. B × P! In the extreme haste of our analysis we had totally overlooked this march with the King and now it might be that this oversight would wreak a bitter revenge.

Since then the main variation had to be rejected, I began to look at eventual deviations from the main line. Perhaps there was something in getting the two united passed pawns by 47. .... K × P? Naturally White must speed with his King to help on the King's side so as to be able to have the eventual threat of B × KtP. So 48. K – Q3, P – Kt4, and if now 49. B × P, then Black eventually obtains a winning position after 49. .... P × B; 50. P – R5, P – R5; 51. K – K2, K – Kt6; 52. K – B1, P – R6, and White will hardly go on into the unpleasant Queen ending by 51. P – R6. This beautiful dream is however thwarted by only one move, namely 49. B – Q2 ch! Now White obtains time for 50. K – K2! after 49. .... K – Kt5 or 49. .... K – B4, and after he has posted his King in front of the pawns he wins again with the B × P sacrifice etc. So Black's position must be regarded as hopeless after 47. B – K1 ch.

But perhaps there had existed somewhat earlier a chance to emerge from the affair with a more or less whole skin? All the variation after 42. P – B4 is forced so only 46. .... P × B instead of 46. .... K × P comes into consideration as a way of rescuing the game in a Queen ending after 47. P – Kt4, K × P. In fact, it would not be so bad after 48. P – Kt5, or 48. P × P, but White has one gigantic, immediately decisive move at his disposal in 48. P – B5! With this the game is finished since after both 48. .... P – R5; 49. BP × P, and 48. .... KtP × P; 49. P – Kt5, White's pawn Queens with check!

My position was then lost and despite numerous attempts I was unable to find where in the variations given above I could have played better. There was nothing else left for me to do but to resume my promenade and await the fatal thrust. Then Pachman came up to me and said, 'You've achieved a marvellous ending,' whereupon I was unable to let matters rest in this way and informed him that 'marvellous' was certainly not the right word, and that I was lost. At first Pachman stared at me in astonishment, but after I had explained the variation to him he had to concede that I was right. With the words 'such things are hardly credible' he left me, shaking his head.

This little episode gave me renewed hope. Even grandmaster Pachman had overlooked the move 47. B – K1 ch, and hence it became clear to me that it was not so easy to find the move. Moreover, my opponent had thought over his next move for more than half an hour – a sign that he had not yet found any clear way.

My hopes however sunk once again to zero when I considered myself what Black could actually play apart from 42. P – B4! The King manoeuvre to Q2 was indeed utterly hopeless, and so White was forced to find the right solution. Thus White needed only to play 42. P – B4, and it would only be necessary, after 42. .... K – B2, to decide whether it would be dangerous to capture the Knight. My opponent thought and thought. By now he had little time left and my hopes rose, since in time trouble anything can happen. At long last, when Fairhurst had only about ten minutes left for his ten remaining moves, there came his reply.

I hurried back to the board and even before I sat down I felt a wave of relief – White's pawn was still standing on KB3! White had in the end determined upon 42. K – K2? and now the whole plan worked as we had shaped it out beforehand:

42. .... P – Kt4; *43*. K – Q2, P – R5; *44*. P × P, P × P. Now *45*. K × Kt, fails on account of *45*. .... P – R6 and so White's King must return: *45*. K– K2, K – B2; *46*. K – B2, K – Kt3; *47*. K – B1, K – Kt4; *48*. K – Kt1 (neither *48*. K – B2, K – B4; *49*. K – B1, Kt – K6 ch; *50*. K – Kt1, P – R6! nor *49*. K – Kt2, Kt – K8 ch, etc. would at all alter the situation), *48*. .... Kt – K8; *49*. B – B1 ch, K – B4; *50*. B – K3, Kt × P ch; *51*. K – B2, K – K5 and White resigned. The win was clear, the shared first prize was assured, but the way to the win had led along the edge of the abyss!

No sooner was the game finished than I hastened to set up the position again and to ask my opponent why he had thought so long and yet had not played *42*. P – B4! It then turned out that the move *47*. B – K1 ch! was not so easy to find. Fairhurst had investigated the whole variation thoroughly as far as *46*. B – B3, and eventually came to the conclusion that Black would win by *46*. .... K × P. Just as we did in our investigations, he had completely overlooked the decisive move *47*. B – K1 ch! The mutual analysis that now ensued strengthened my conviction that Black's position could not be saved. Fairhurst sat gazing at the position for a long time, unable to understand how one could overlook such a move despite a thorough study of the position.

This example may serve as a proof that analysis of an adjourned game is not so simple, but that it demands the utmost accuracy. It is characteristic that the move *47*. B – K1 ch! was overlooked by both sides, not on account of its being difficult to find, but because we deemed the position after *46*. .... K × P to be so simple and clear that there was not much to be examined thereafter. In this particular case I did not have much time at my disposal and I discovered the move when I had little time left for thought. It is always difficult to analyse a position exhaustively, even when it is not particularly complicated. It is therefore quite natural that, on resumption of play, one often stumbles upon unpleasant surprises that turn one's adjourned analysis completely upside down.

In the previous example we saw what subtle traps often lie concealed in adjourned positions. One must be extremely careful to check the analysed variations many times so as not to fall victim to lethal surprises. Yet another example of the matter is to be found in the game Tal–Keres from the fourth Candidates' Tournament at Belgrade, 1959. But this time, whereas the surprising point in the game against Fairhurst went undetected, I succeeded against Tal in finding a diabolical trap in my adjournment analysis. Had I not made it, then the game might well have had quite another result. But now let us see what occurred.

After White's forty-first move there arose the position shown in the diagram.

Keres

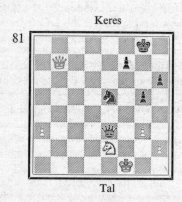

81

Tal

There was time trouble on both sides, and I had sacrificed my last Queen-side pawn on Kt2. Perhaps these tactics were not the safest, but they seemed to yield good chances. Now I had to seal the move. After a short period of reflection I made the natural move (on which I had already decided earlier).

    41. . . . .   Kt – Q6

It was with this position as my starting-point that I began my adjournment analysis. My opponent's first move was not difficult to find, since the mating threat on KB2 left him but little choice.

    42. Q – B8 ch

As is easy to see, the only move. After *42*. Q – KKt2, Black could proceed very simply *42*. .... P – Kt5! after which his opponent would be practically paralysed. White would only be able to move his QRP, and after *43*. P – QR4, K – Kt2; *44*. P – R5, Black wins by *44*. .... Q – Q7!; *45*. Q – K4, Q – K8 ch; *46*. K – Kt2, Q – B7 ch, followed by mate. Queen checks on R8 and Kt8 also lead to similar continuations.

> *42*. ....   K – Kt2
> *43*. Q – KB5!

Here the Queen is beautifully placed, since it not only prevents the mate on B2 but also stands ready for an eventual attack on the enemy King. However, Black can, despite the reduced material, continue his attack with undiminished force.

> *43*. ....   -   Q – Q7!

Now he threatened to win the Knight by *44*. .... Q – K8 ch, and hence again White only has a restricted choice.

> *44*. Kt – Q4!

It should be observed that Black's last move also entails a small disadvantage, since White's Knight has this fine square at its disposal. Despite this, I at first regarded the Knight move as inadequate and comparatively easy to refute, even supposing it could offer any real resistance. As however we shall come to perceive in the sequel, the position, seemingly so simple and easy, conceals a number of surprises.

White has in any case nothing better, since other moves clearly lose without any further struggle. Black's threat is of course *44*. .... Q – K8 ch, winning the Knight, and this piece must therefore either move or be protected. The defence *44*. Q – K4, Q – K8 ch; *45*. K – Kt2, Q – B7 ch; followed by *46*. .... Q – B8 ch, or also *44*. Q – B3, Q – Q8 ch; *45*. K – Kt2, Kt – K8 ch leads to an immediate loss. The one retreat for the Knight, *44*. Kt – Kt1, also loses after *44*. .... Q – Q8 ch; *45*. K – Kt2, Q – B7 ch!, e.g. *46*. K – B1, Q – Kt8 ch followed by *47*. .... Kt – B5 ch, or *46*. K – B3, Q – B7 ch; *47*. K – Kt4

(or *47.* K – K4, Kt – B4 ch; *48.* K – K5, P – B3 ch etc.),
47. .... P – R4 ch; *48.* K × KtP, P – B3 ch and White loses
his Queen. The Black attack proves to be surprisingly dangerous.

44.	Q – K8 ch

But White's position turns out to possess an almost incredible
capacity for resistance. There always exists only one narrow way
for Black to proceed if he wishes to retain an attack and set difficult problems to his adversary. The plausible continuation
44. .... Q – Q8 ch; *45.* K – Kt2, Kt – K8 ch leads, for
example, after 46. K – B2, Q × Kt ch; *47.* K × Kt, to a Queen
ending which would only give Black highly problematic winning prospects. I deemed it best however to hold this continuation in reserve, in case the attack in the chief variation should
not lead to any clear result.

45. K – Kt2	Q – K6!

It was this position that I had in mind when I began my
analysis of the method of attack by *43.* .... Q – Q7. Apparently White has emerged from his critical situation comparatively easily, since his King is for the moment secure against
mating threats, and the attack on the Knight on Q4 can be
parried in similar fashion. If, however, one investigates the
position more thoroughly and tries to get some concrete protection for the Knight, then new difficulties suddenly emerge. The
enemy possibilities must first of all be checked with the utmost
exactness before one can decide upon a continuation for the
attack.

46. Q – Q5!

Again the only move. The Knight cannot be guarded in any
other way, since after *46.* Q – Kt4, or *46.* Q – Q7, *46.* ....
Q – B7 ch would lead to mate.

It remains then to be seen if the Knight cannot quite simply
move away. There are five squares at its disposal and we will
now investigate all the possibilities.

(1) 46. Kt – B3, Q – K7 ch; 47. K – R3 (or 47. K – Kt1, Q – B7 ch etc.), 47. .... Kt – B7 ch; 48. K – Kt2, Kt – Q8 dis ch! 49. K – R3, Q – B8 ch winning the Queen.

(2) 46. Kt – B2, Q – K7 ch; followed by 47. .... Q × Kt and wins.

(3) 46. Kt – Kt3, Q – K7 ch; 47. K – R3 (or 47. K – Kt1, Q – Q8 ch followed by 48. .... Q × Kt, etc.), 47. .... Kt – B5 ch! followed either by mate or win of the Queen.

(4) 46. Kt – B6, Q – Q7 ch; 47. K – R3 (or 47. K – Kt1, Q – B8 ch; 48. Q – B1, Q – B4 ch winning the Knight), 47. .... Kt – B7 ch; 48. K – Kt2, Kt – Kt5 dis ch; 49. K – R3 (Black wins the Queen after 49. K – B3, Q – B7 ch; 50. K × Kt, P – R4 ch; 51. K × KtP, P – B3 ch), 49. .... P – R4, and mate on KR2 can no longer be averted.

(5) 46. Kt – Kt5, Q – K7 ch (46. .... Q – Q7 ch also wins, as in Variation 4), 47. K – Kt1 (after 47. K – R3, there again follows 47. .... Kt – B5 ch and after 47. K – R1, Kt – K8! Mate is not to be prevented), 47. .... Kt – K4! 48. Kt – Q4, Q – Q8 ch winning the Knight.

Thoroughly convincing variations! The text-move seemed to me at first to be hardly any better, since now apparently Black wins by force in a few moves.

46. ....   Q – B7 ch

It is indeed surprising that Black is unable to obtain an immediately decisive gain of material. However one tries, there always exists a way, narrow it is true, but passable, by which White can escape from Black's clutches. Very enticing seems 46. .... Q – Q7 ch so as to be able to continue after 47. K – R1 (or R3), with 47. .... Kt – B7 ch; 48. K – Kt2 (or 48. K – Kt1, Q – K8 ch; 49. K – Kt2, Q – R8 ch, etc.), 48. .... Kt – Q8 dis ch; 49. K – B3 (or R3), P – Kt5 ch and Black wins. White plays, however, 47. K – B3! and whatsoever one tries there exists no way of continuing the attack.

47. K – R3   Q – B8 ch
48. K – Kt4

Keres

82

Tal

Now the critical position is reached. In my analysis I got as far as this after some tries and then devoted myself to other possibilities, since it all seemed clear here. Black can indeed play *48. .... P – R4 ch; 49. K × KtP (or 49. K × RP, Q – R6 ch; 50. K × P, P – B3 mate!), 49. .... Q – B3 ch; 50. K × P, Kt – K4;* and how can White now parry the mating threats on R6 and Kt6? Only *51. Kt – K6 ch* seems to be possible, but then Black wins easily after *51. .... P × Kt; 52. Q – Kt7 ch, Kt – B2,* etc. since White's King is in a mating net from which there is no escape.

Thus far everything was clear and logical. I also investigated the possibilities of White being able to play in another way earlier on and found in every case that it was a simple win for Black. Most variations were forced, too, so the subsequent checking of them was extremely easy. Satisfied and content, I set the position on one side in the conviction that I had a forced win in the making.

However, following my usual custom, I undertook a further check of the position before I went to the playing-room to continue the game. Everything was in perfect order. Yet once again I looked into the possibilities after the Knight sacrifice, *51. Kt – K6 ch,* but could not find any saving clause for White. Everything ran on oiled wheels.

And then I suddenly got a shock! To my horror I perceived a hole in my analysis which threatened to turn all my work upside down. White need not in fact sacrifice his Knight by *51. Kt – K6 ch?* but could parry all the threats by the surprising move *51. Q – Q6!!* Then the exchange of Queens would be forced and not Black but White would win the game. An obscure move, of the type that is liable to be overlooked in adjournment analysis, not to mention actual play.

Once over the first shock I began to study the position with renewed ardour. If there did not exist any immediate win, then at least there must be some method of play that would assure Black of a decisive advantage. But it seemed as though the position was bewitched, and however I tried there was always an adequate defence for White. I began to lose my temper with the position and still could find no decisive line.

48.		Kt – B7 ch!

In the end I decided upon this check, since I could not find anything better. After *48.* .... *Q – Q8 ch* White could not, it is true, intervene with a piece on B3, but after *49. K – B5*, Black gets no further. Other moves are scarcely worth considering.

49. K – B5		Q – Q6 ch

Nothing else really comes into question. After *49.* .... *Q – Kt8 ch; 50. K – K5*, Black achieves nothing either with *50.* .... *Kt – Kt5 ch; 51. K – Q6, Q – Kt1 ch; 52. K – B5*, or with *50.* .... *Kt – Q6 ch; 51. K – Q6, Q – Kt1 ch; 52. K – B6*. It is almost incredible, but still a fact that none of the various discovered checks lead to any tangible result. After *49.* .... *Kt – Q8 dis ch* White has the one saving clause *50. Q – B3!* and other discovered checks offer even less prospects.

50. K – K5		Kt – Kt5 ch
51. K – Q6		Q × RP ch

This was all that I could obtain from the long and patient labour of analysis. As my luck would have it, this was enough for the win, since Black soon wins yet another pawn and then only has to beat back a last despairing attack. It is however even to this day an enigma for me that I could not find more in the position, but despite the most meticulous analysis I could never succeed in finding any stronger continuation. If anything further should be found in it then I am absolutely sure that the continuation must be very surprising and extremely well concealed.

The 'incredulity' is however prolonged, as Black is not able to force the exchange of Queens. All the time, White has only one move at his disposal, but it is sufficient.

    52. K – B7   Q – K2 ch
    53. K – B8   Kt – K6

With this move I ended my analysis, since I regarded the position as won in practice. Instead of the Knight move, Black could naturally also take the second pawn and continue with *53.* .... Q – K1 ch; *54.* K – Kt7, Kt × P. I did not, however, want to move my Knight so far away from the theatre of war and chose the text-move on the grounds that White's open King's position and his insecurely placed pieces would ensure the win for Black. The home analysis was at an end and now I had to await the resumption of play.

The game, when play was continued, did in fact proceed in accordance with the analysis, and soon we had reached the position given below. Even though this does not pertain directly to our theme, it may be of interest to see how the game finished.

Keres

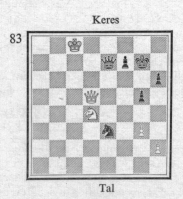

83

Tal

    54. Q – Kt5

Naturally not *54. Kt – B5* ch, on account of *54. ....* Kt × Kt; *55.* Q × Kt, Q – K3 ch and Black wins.

| *54. ....* | Q – K5 |
| *55.* Q – Kt2 | K – Kt3 |

It is very difficult for White here. He must not only avoid exchange of Queens, which is not so easy to do, bearing in mind his open King's position, but he must also take precautions against his opponent's advance on the King's wing.

56. Q – Kt6 ch	P – B3
57. Kt – K6	Kt – B5
58. Q – R6	Kt – K4

Now the Knight is beautifully centralized and once again a Queen exchange is threatened. The possible sacrifice by *59. Kt – B8* ch, K – B2; *60. Q – K6* ch, K × Kt; *61. Q × P* ch, is insufficient on account of *61. ....* Kt – B2.

| *59.* Kt – B7 | Q – B7 |

Now Black has got so far as to force White to lose further material on the King's wing. The game approaches its second crisis.

| *60.* Q – Q6 | |

Nor would *60. P – R4*, have been of any use because of *60. ....* Q – B4 ch; *61.* K – Kt8 (or *61.* K – Kt7, Q – B6 ch; followed by Q × P, etc.), *61. ....* Kt – Q2 ch; *62.* K – R7, Q – B7 ch when White would lose the pawn under much more unfavourable circumstances than in the game. With the text-move he hopes at least to obtain the initiative for some time in compensation for the pawn, and he does in fact succeed in driving back his opponent to the defensive.

| *60. ....* | Q × P |
| *61.* Kt – Q5 | Q – KB7 |

It would have been simpler to have captured at once on KKt6, since the protection of the KBP deprives the Black Queen of further active possibilities.

62. K – Kt7

After long thought White refrains from the immediate *62.* Q – K6, on account of the possibility *62.* .... Q – B4 ch; *63.* K – Kt7, Q – B1, when Black's King would be completely safe from attack. After the text-move *63.* Q – K6 is again in the air and hence Black decides to clarify matters.

62.	Q × P!
63. Q × P ch	K – R4
64. Q – K6	

White continues to provide his opponent with the greatest possible difficulties. Black's King is tethered to the pawn on R3, and the threat is *65.* Kt – B6 ch, K – R5; *66.* Kt – K4, followed by the capture of the pawn.

64.	Kt – Kt5
65. Kt – K7	

On an immediate *65.* Q – B7 ch, K – R5 and only then *66.* Kt – K7, Black can reply *66.* .... K – R6, since *67.* Q – R5 ch, K – Kt7, would result in White's Queen getting out of play. With the move played White again presents Black with an unpleasant threat.

65.	Q – B6 ch
66. K – B8	

After *66.* K – B7, K – R5 Black would threaten a check on K4 that would be highly remunerative. But the text-move has other drawbacks.

66.	K – R5
67. Kt – B5 ch	K – R6
68. K – Q8	

Now it becomes apparent that *68.* Kt × P will not do because of *68.* .... Q – B1 ch followed by *69.* .... Q × Kt. Once Black has overcome the last troublesome threat his win is clear at long last.

68.	P – R4
69. Q – KKt6	Kt – K4

70. Q – K6	Kt – Kt5
71. Q – KKt6	Kt – K4

Black is once again in time trouble. The repetition of moves is made so as to enable him to get through the time control on his seventy-second move.

72. Q – K6	Q – Q6 ch
73. Kt – Q4 dis ch	

Unfortunately forced, since after 73. K – K8, Black wins simply by 73. .... Q – Q2 ch!; 74. Q × Q, Kt × Q; 75. K × Kt, P – Kt5, etc. No better is the try 73. Kt – Q6 dis ch, on account of 73. .... Kt – Kt5.

73.	Kt – Kt5
74. Q – Q5	Kt – B7!

The simplest way to win.

75. K – B8	P – R5
76. Q – K5	Q – K5
77. Q – B6	Q – B5
78. Kt – B5	Kt – K5
79. Q – K6	Q – Kt5
resigns.	

There is no longer any defence against the threat of 80. .... Kt – Kt6.

A fighting game of high quality. It shows that even in a seemingly hopeless position one can put up a stern resistance, provided one possesses the necessary powers of resourcefulness. From our particular standpoint too, this example is most instructive. It demonstrates yet once again how carefully one must analyse an adjourned position and how one must check over and over again the various possibilities, so as to illuminate all the finesses in the position, thereby avoiding disagreeable, possibly deadly, occurrences when play is resumed.

So far we have only shown games in which one side succeeds in finding a satisfactory continuation in his adjournment analysis. It often happens however that one gets a game adjourned in a difficult position and is only concerned with trying to find a way to save it. Generally speaking, such positions are more difficult to analyse since practice shows that it is easier to attack than to defend. Furthermore, it makes a considerable difference whether one is searching for a good attacking continuation for oneself or for one's opponent. It seems that one usually discovers one's own possibilities much more easily and that one must often vex one's head for a long time to discern the opponent's best method of attack.

In order to give the reader an example of this nature we will study the position in the following diagram, which is from a game Keres–Smyslov, Parnu, 1947, after Black's fortieth move.

Smyslov

84

Keres

The very first glance shows how terribly difficult the position is for White. His pieces are practically stalemated and Black needs only to create for himself a passed pawn on the QR file in order to decide the struggle in his favour. In order to do this he must play his Knight to KR4 where, as it happens, it stood earlier in the game but had been mistakenly played away by Smyslov. After this it would be impossible to prevent the advance P – QKt4, since White's King is tethered to the task of protecting the KBP and through this all counter-play is nullified.

What then can White do in the diagram position? It is clear

that *41.* Kt × R, P × Kt; *42.* R – KR1, will not do, since then Black can immediately force a decision in his favour by either *42.* .... Kt – Kt6 or *42.* .... P – Kt6 followed by *43.* .... Kt – B7. So Black must remain passive, temporarily at any rate. After the faulty manoeuvre with the Knight to K5 White's situation has become in fact a little easier, since thereby he has obtained the opportunity of bringing his Knight to K3, where it will be well placed and attack the pawns on Q4 and B4. This chance must of course be immediately utilized and therefore I sealed a move that freed the K3 square for the Knight.

41. K – Q3   Kt – B7 ch

In what follows I not only show the processes of thought and the variations that I examined in my analysis, but I also give at the same time the actual progress of the game. This last, it should be observed, went on right till the end in accordance with my adjournment analysis, and the final position obtained was the one I had already envisaged away from the board.

The text-move is not of any great importance and does not pertain to my opponent's winning plan. It is merely a feeler to find out if White is going to allow himself to be lured into the blunder *42.* K – K2?, Kt – R6!

42. K – K3   Kt – K5

Apparently Smyslov had discovered in his adjournment analysis that the attempt to win by *42.* .... Kt – Q8 ch; *43.* K – Q2, Kt – Kt7 would not be sufficient. In reply White could obtain adequate counter-play by *44.* Kt × P, Kt – B5 ch; *45.* K – Q3, P – Kt4; *46.* P × P ch, K × P; *47.* Kt × P, since then Black's Rook on KR7 would be too passively placed for an attack. Moreover, no exhaustive analysis is necessary to convince oneself that the Rook exchange by *42.* .... R – R8; *43.* R × R, Kt × R; *44.* K – Q2, affords no win for Black.

43. K – Q3   R – R1

Black can no longer prevent the counter-attack by Kt – K3 and must regroup his pieces so as to fit in with the new situation. Since the Rook has nothing much to do on R7 Black thinks of placing it on the K file, while the Knight may, as the occasion arises, be played to QB5. With this, however, White's pieces also gain freedom of movement, a circumstance of which use must be made immediately.

As we shall soon see, the White Rook later obtains a stake on the KR file and gets in a position from whence it exerts an uncomfortable bind on the sixth rank. So there comes into question the possibility of only playing the Rook as far as the third rank so as to deprive White's Rook of some, at any rate, of the pressure on the KR file. But the move *43. . . . . R – R3* is tied up with other drawbacks. After *44. Kt – K3, Kt – Q3* White can in fact play *45. P – B4!* and then it becomes apparent that Black, after *45. . . . . P × P ch; 46. Kt × P, Kt × Kt; 47. K × Kt*, cannot occupy the K file by *47. . . . . R – K3?* on account of P – Q5 ch, etc.

    44. Kt – K3   Kt – Q3
    45. R – K1!

White must not waste time by trying to restore material equality in capturing the pawn on KKt3. Black would then, in fact, sacrifice yet another pawn and after this would have his pieces posted in most active positions which, in conjunction with the passed pawn on the QR file, should be decisive. The concrete variation is as follows: *45. Kt – B1, Kt – B5! 46. Kt × P, R – K1; 47. Kt × P, P – Kt4; 48. P × P ch, K × P*, and White would hardly be able to hold the ending. Only by developing the power of his pieces to their fullest extent can White hope to save the game.

But the text-move also threatens once more *46. P – B4*, which would not have done at once because of *45. . . . . P × P ch; 46. Kt × P, Kt × Kt; 47. K × Kt, R – K1*, with a won Rook ending for Black.

    45. . . . .   R – K1

Otherwise Black can hardly make any progress. Now White naturally takes immediate possession of the open KR file.

    46. R – KR1!   R – K5

Undoubtedly Black's best chance. He must at once attack the enemy pawns on the King's wing, since otherwise White has nothing to fear as his pieces are beginning to look very actively placed. I had analysed this position exhaustively and in the end came to the conclusion that the attack initiated by the text-move was the only one that gave Black prospects of success or that could indeed pose any problems to White.

47. R – R6!

Only a desperate counter-attack can save White. One might think that the more obvious *47. R – KB1*, or *47. R – QKt1*, would also suffice, but in the end I rejected both possibilities. After *47. R – KB1*, Black can in fact play *47. .... Kt – B5; 48. Kt × BP, P – Kt4; 49. P × P ch, K × P,* when his pieces are ideally placed and the RP will eventually prove decisive. If, however, White tries *47. R – QKt1*, so as to meet *47. .... R × P?* with *48. R × P ch*, then Black continues in very similar fashion with *47. .... Kt – B5!* and plays after *48. Kt × BP, R – K3!* In this singular *Zugzwang* position White can only move his Rook and then Black penetrates to the back ranks or else arrives at P – QKt4 and we are faced with a position round about the same as that which arises after *47. R – KB1*.

These variations, which appear here so convincingly simple in retrospect, are in actual fact not so easy to find. One must literally busy oneself uniquely with the position before one can discern the subtle finesses and the perils that are attached to them.

The move played is at all events much more sure than the rest, and even if great complications arise in the ensuing play, one should still be able to analyse them with great accuracy. The pinning of the Knight noticeably lessens Black's attacking chances and leaves only a small path open to him by which he can build up his initiative.

47.	R × P
48. P – B4	

In this advance lies White's saving counter-play.

48.	P × P ch

An immediate *48. . . . . R – B7* scarcely offered better winning chances on account of *49. P × P ch, K– Q2; 50. R –R7 ch*; and Black will not find it easy to escape the checks. If his King retreats to the back rank, then White can drive it to the K file and after that threaten the Knight with *R – R6*. It is difficult to see how Black can then get any further.

49. Kt × P	R – B6 ch!

This is the chief point of Black's attack, by which he wins an important tempo. Some commentators expressed the opinion after the game that this check came as a surprise to me and that only after long thought and painful labour could I then find a way to save myself. This is correct only in so far that I now once again checked over the consequences of the text-move, as I am always accustomed to do when I play variations I have discovered during adjournment analysis. Experience shows that adjournment analysis cannot be checked often enough. That this check came as a surprise to me is naturally nonsense. As I said earlier, I had already arrived at the final position that resulted over the board in the game in my adjournment analysis and therefore I must certainly have reckoned with the move played.

Smyslov

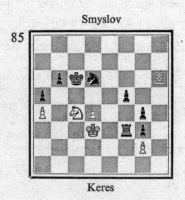

85

Keres

50. Kt – K3

The variation 50. K – K2, R – B7 ch; 51. K – Q3, etc. would transpose back into the game. On the other hand, the continuation 50. P × R, P – Kt7; 51. Kt × Kt, P – Kt8 = Q; 52. Kt × P dis ch, followed by 53. P × P, would merely give Black winning chances. Even 51. .... K – B2 would come into consideration so as to answer 52. Kt × P with 52. .... P × P.

| 50. .... | R – B7 |

Neither the exchange sacrifice 50. .... R × Kt ch; 51. K × R, K – Q4; 52. K – B4, nor the Rook sacrifice 50. ... P – B5; 51. P × R, P × P; 52. Kt – B4! would be dangerous for White. Now, however, there threatens quite simply 51. .... K – Q2.

51. Kt – B4!

The simplest continuation to maintain equality. The following moves are more or less forced.

| 51. .... | R × P |
| 52. R × Kt ch | |

It is interesting to observe that 52. Kt × Kt, also seems possible. After 52. .... R – Q7 ch; 53. K × R, P – Kt7 White plays 54. Kt × P dis ch, and since the Black King must not be played to the K file, so as to avoid the drawing checks, it must wander to QR3. There would then follow, however, 54. .... K – Kt2; 55. R – R7 ch, K – R3; 56. Kt – Q6! P – Kt8 = Q; 57. Kt – Kt5, and White should obtain a draw since in reply to the Queen checks he can oscillate with his King from Q2 to Q1, etc. The text-move is however much surer.

| 52. .... | K – B2 |
| 53. P – Q5! | |

This pawn not only assures White's Rook the necessary checks on the sixth rank, but eventually threatens itself to advance further and thus to become a most powerful factor in the game.

53. ....   R – Kt8

The move *54. .... R – Q7 ch* would be innocuous on account of *54. K × R, P – Kt7; 55. R – B6 ch*, when White would obtain a draw by perpetual check. Similarly *53. .... R – KB7* is without prospects because of *54. R – B6 ch*. Now Black's King can escape the checks with difficulty only, e.g. *54. .... K – Q1* (after *54. .... K – Kt1* there could follow *55. P – Q6*); *55. R – Q6 ch, K – K2; 56. R – K6 ch*, and now *56. .... K – B1* will not do because of *57. P – Q6*. However, if Black tries *56. .... K – B2*, then there could follow *57. Kt – K5 ch, K – Kt2; 58. R – K7 ch, K – B3; 59. R – K6 ch, K – Kt4; 60. P – Q6!* and White even gets winning chances (*60. .... R – B8; 61. Kt – B4!* etc.). The text-move is undoubtedly Black's best.

54. R – B6 ch   K – Q1
55. R – Q6 ch   K – B2

Smyslov

86

Keres

Black allows himself to be contented at once with a draw. He could have given his opponent a much bigger headache by *55. .... K – K2; 56. R – K6 ch, K – B2!* Thereafter he has the most disagreeable threat of *57. .... P – Kt7*, and White must defend himself with the utmost accuracy if he wishes to avoid getting a disadvantage. After, for example, *57. Kt – K5* ch, K – Kt2, or *57.* Kt – Q6 ch, K – Kt1! White's attempt to obtain an immediate draw by checking would not prove adequate.

It should not be so difficult to demonstrate that the position, even in this case, would be level. From the various possibilities I will select two simple methods of play, which, in my opinion, would enable Black to maintain equality.

In the first place we ought to look at *57.* Kt – Q6 ch, K – Kt1; *58.* K – K3! so as to meet *58. ....* P – Kt7 with *59.* K – B2. Since *58. ....* R – K8 ch? *59.* K – B4, R × R; *60.* P × R, K – B1; *61.* K – K5! would eventually end in a win for White, Black, practically speaking, is forced to play *58. ....* R – KB8. Now there follows, however, *59.* R – K8 ch, K – R2; *60.* R – K7 ch, K – Kt3; *61.* R – K6 ch, K – R4; *62.* Kt – B7, R – K8 ch; *63.* K – Q3, R × R; *64.* P × R, P – Kt7 (or *64. ....* K – Kt3; *65.* Kt – Q6, K – B3; *66.* P – K7! etc.) *65.* P – K7, P – Kt8 = Q; *66.* P – K8 = Q, with about a level ending.

The other way is still simpler. White can continue with *57.* Kt – Q6 ch, K – Kt1; *58.* Kt × P! and after *58. ....* P – Kt7; *59.* R – Kt6 ch, K – B1; *60.* R × KKtP, R – Q8 ch; *61.* K – B4, P – Kt8 = Q; *62.* R × Q, R × R; *63.* K – Kt5, he can reach an ending which can be held without difficulty.

There exist perhaps other ways that retain equality, but these two should suffice. In any case Black could have allowed himself to be shown them, but probably he thought he had had enough excitement for the day, and therefore contented himself with the draw.

56. R – B6 ch	K – Q1
57. R – Q6 ch	

Drawn.

As I have already said, I had reached this position before in my adjournment analysis. So the work at home had borne good fruit and the game ran exactly along lines that I regarded as best for Black. As we saw, White's defence was not so easy to conduct, and one would hardly venture to believe that the game could have been held had play proceeded on the board immediately without intermission.

The analysis given above shows once again with what accuracy one must examine adjourned positions. Such a move as *49. .... R – B6 ch!* is easily overlooked, and yet the whole game centres round this move. Work, labour, and toil yet once more – these words constitute the motto for adjourned games!

With these examples we have given a comparatively full picture of the difficulties that chess-masters experience away from the board at the adjournment of a tournament game. To finish I should like to show a position that has left an indelible mark on my memory. It occurred in the Chess Olympiad at Moscow, 1956, in my game against Rejfir and is remarkable in that despite the highly complicated nature of the position it is possible to analyse it in terms of a well-nigh forced winning line.

After time trouble on both sides during which sundry lamentable mistakes occurred, the game was adjourned after Black's fortieth move in the following complicated position.

Keres

87

Rejfir

In time trouble White had conjured up some very unpleasant threats against the Black King, but the far advanced pawn on Q7 ruined his hope of saving the position. Despite everything, however, the position concealed many finesses that had to be surmounted before the situation became more or less clear. Black's immediate threat was *41. . . . . P – B3*, and hence it was not so difficult to work out White's sealed move.

I was soon able to establish that the desperate attack *41. Q × KBP, R × Kt ch; 42. P × R, Q × P ch* followed by *43. . . . . Q × P ch* and *44. . . . . P – Q8 = Q* would not lead to a draw by perpetual check and so, in practice, only a King move or else *41. Q – Q3* came into question. The Queen move was then the most natural, and so as to exclude other possibilities as rapidly as possible I began first of all by analysing the possible King moves.

Moves such as *41. K – R1*, and *41. K – R3*, could be rejected comparatively quickly, because then there would come *41. . . . . R × Kt; 42. P × R, Q × KKtP*, which results in a position in which there is no good defence against the threat of *43. . . . . P – B4* followed by the Queen exchange on Kt5. Thus there remained only *41. K – B1* to be investigated, but there too the answer was easy to find. In the first place *41. . . . . Q – K2* with the threat of *P – B4* is good enough and in the second, fully adequate would be *41. . . . . R × Kt; 42. P × R, Q –Q5; 43. Q – Q1, Q × QBP ch; 44. K – Kt2, Q – Q4 ch.* Black would thereby arrive at the same position as in the main variation; he would only have captured, in passing, the pawn on QB5.

So the sealed move was not difficult to find, since nothing but a Queen move scarcely came into consideration.

    41. Q – Q3

Nor had Black so many different moves from which to choose, since, on account of the mating threat on R2 he must either give back the exchange on Kt4 or else defend himself by *41. . . . . P – B4*. In the latter case, however, White could by *42. Q × QP* simply dispose of the strong passed pawn; and therefore it was clear that a winning attempt could only be made in a Queen ending after an exchange sacrifice.

    41. . . . .   R × Kt ch
    42. P × R

Now there has arisen an extraordinarily interesting Queen ending that is a real pleasure to analyse. It is clear that the passed pawn on Q7 ensures a clear advantage to Black; but the burning question is whether this advantage is sufficient for a win. In order to be in a position to answer this question correctly one must carry out an exhaustive and systematic investigation into the ending.

It needs merely a first glance to convince one that the win is only possible if White's King can be kept away from the passed pawn and White's Queen can be forced to the passive square on Q1. The approach of White's King would naturally lead to the loss of the passed pawn, and likewise Black can hardly allow an active White Queen in view of the open nature of his King's position. One soon comes to the conclusion that the respective Queen positions on Black's Q6 and White's Q1 constitute the right final objective for Black.

For this reason 42. .... Q × P ch must be speedily rejected, since White could then occupy the square K2 with his King, whereupon his opponent's winning chances are highly problematical. So Black must at first leave the pawn in peace and direct his efforts to forcing White's Queen to Q1.

42.		Q – Q5!
43. Q – K2		K – R2

As can be easily seen, the last moves were forced. Now White's Queen must go to Q1 and Black obtains the desired Queen position on Q1 and Q6.

44. Q – Q1		Q – Q6!

With this the first phase in the end game is completed. As can be seen, White's Queen is completely stalemated and White can now make only King or pawn moves. So Black can prepare his plans in the utmost tranquillity since no interruption on the part of his adversary is to be feared in the near future. Now the question is: how can Black strengthen his position?

THE ART OF ANALYSIS

Keres

88

Rejfir

It very soon becomes apparent that the attempt to force the
pawn promotion by means of the Queen alone does not lead to
the desired goal. If Black plays, for example, *44. .... Q – K5
ch* on his next move so as to be able to continue after *45.
K – R2* with *45. .... Q – K8*, then White plays *46. Q – B3*, or
46. Q – B2 ch, K – Kt1; 47. Q – B5, and the pawn promotion
cannot work. However, if Black takes the Kt pawn after
45. .... Q – R5 ch; 46. K – Kt2, Q × KtP ch then there
follows *47. K – B1*, and Black can no longer prevent White's
King from getting to K2. So the Queen by itself will not suffice.

It is also easy to see that Black cannot achieve anything with
his pawns, and thus eventually one is reduced to the conviction
that the cooperation of one's own King is necessary for the
win. But how can the King be brought near the QP when White
can play P – R7 as soon as the King leaves the right-hand
corner of the board? It becomes apparent that the win, despite
Black's overwhelming position, can only be obtained if Black
can succeed in breaking the enemy pawn chain by P – B3, and
thus set his King free so as to penetrate eventually with decisive
effect into the centre.

Thus in theory the winning plan was clear, but in practice it
was not so easy. One always had to bear in mind that the enemy
Queen was liable to come into action suddenly and bring about
a draw by perpetual check. I succeeded, however, in solving the
problem satisfactorily.

223

45. P – Kt3

Protecting the QBP once and for all. The weakening of the QB3 square does not matter much, since White always has at his disposal Q – K2 as a parry against an eventual Q – B6: *45.* Q – R5, Q × P is worse.

45. . . . .   P – B3!

As has already been observed, this breaking of the pawn chain is Black's only possibility of getting any further. In addition it prevents eventual counter-play by Q – QR1.

46. P × P

Here, too, the sortie *46.* Q – R5, would be innocuous on account of the simple reply *46.* . . . . P × P! since White has no perpetual check at his disposal. An interesting line then would be *47.* Q – B7 ch, K × P; *48.* Q – B8 ch, K – R4; *49.* Q – K8 ch! (after *49.* Q – B7 ch, K – R5, White has no more checks), *49.* . . . . K – R5; *50.* P – B3! (the best chance; after *50.* Q – R8 ch, K – Kt5; *51.* Q – B8 ch, Q – B4; *52.* P – B3 ch, K – B5, Black's King escapes via K6; after the text-move, however, mate is threatened on KR8, and this, curiously enough, is not so easy to parry) *50.* . . . Q × P ch! the only continuation!) *51.* K × Q, P – Q8 = Q ch; *52.* K – B2, Q – Q7 ch; *53.* K – Kt1 (after *53.* K – B1, Black wins at once by K – Kt6), *53.* . . . . . . Q – Q5 ch! *54.* K – Kt2, Q – Kt7 ch, and Black wins. After *55.* K – B1, Q – Kt8 ch followed by *56.* . . . . Q × P ch would lead to an easily won ending with two pawns more, and after *55.* K – B3, P – Kt5 ch; *56.* K – K3, Q – Q5 ch; *57.* K – K2, K – Kt6 is decisive. The variations are not particularly complicated, but despite that they require exact calculation.

Since the Queen sortie fails to attain its objective, *46.* P – B4 must be considered. It is, however, easy to establish that this advance either here or later only makes Black's task easier, since Black can gain possession of the vital K6 square and entirely paralyse White's pieces. Black could then win most simply by *46.* . . . . Q – K5 ch; *47.* K – R3 (*47.* K – B2, Q × P ch loses at once for White) *47.* . . . . Q × KBP, by which he would attain a position similar to that in the game with the difference that the pawn on KB2 would be missing.

  46. ....   K × P
  47. P – B7

White at once surrenders the pawn of his own free will, since otherwise Black captures it by K – Kt3 and K × P. After *47. P – B4*, there would similarly have followed *47. .... K – Kt3*, since after *48. Q – Kt4 ch, K × P; 49. Q – Kt5 ch, K – B2*, there are no more checks and Black wins.

  47. ....   K – Kt2
  48. K – Kt1

This passive defence is White's best chance of still putting up some further resistance. Nor would the attempt to obtain perpetual check by *48. Q – Kt4 ch*, lead to anything now. After *48. .... K × P; 49. Q – B4 ch, K – K3*, Black's King escapes to the Queen's wing and finds a refuge on Kt3. As an example of one of the possible variations: *50. Q – Kt4 ch, K – Q3; 51. Q – B4 ch* (after *51. Q – Q1*, Black can transpose to the main variation, since he can get his King to KR4 via K2, B3, and Kt4), *51. .... K – Q2; 52. Q – KB7 ch, K – B1; 53. Q – K8 ch, K – Kt2; 54. Q – K7 ch, K – Kt3*, and White must resign.

  48. ....   K × P
  49. K – Kt2

Keres

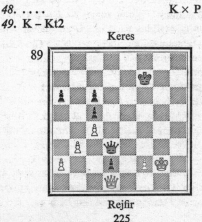

Rejfir

With this the second stage in Black's plan to win is achieved. He has now only to work out how his King can be best employed. Firstly there comes into consideration the march of the King to the Queen's wing so as to penetrate via QKt5 and QR6. This plan is however difficult to execute, since by playing P – QR3 at the right moment White can prevent it, and in addition the KBP may advance if the King is taken too far away. It is naturally possible that even this plan may lead to positive results, but it does not altogether give one a logical impression.

An idea that is much more likely to attain its aim is therefore to advance with the King either in the centre or along the King's wing. The advance in the centre, however, would encounter great practical difficulties, since the only possible way via K4 and Q5 is extremely difficult to traverse. When Black's King goes to K4, then White gives check with his Queen on KR5 and Black's King cannot get to Q5 on account of Q – R8 ch with a draw.

It remains therefore only to examine the possibilities of an advance on the King's wing.

It is very obvious that Black can allow his King to proceed along the diagonal Q1 – KR5 and reach R5 without having to fear enemy checks. Once the King does stand on R5 then the threat of Q – R6 ch, followed by Q – Kt5 ch and exchange of Queens becomes acute. If White keeps his King on KKt1 then he can neither budge with his King nor Queen without incurring immediate loss. So at last we have a clear winning position, which is also seemingly easy to attain.

Let us, once and for all, see how Black can reach this goal. The King can get to R5 without being diverted in any way: *49.* .... K – B3; *50.* K – Kt1, K – Kt4; *51.* K – Kt2, K – R5; *52.* K – Kt1, P – R4; *53.* P – R4. If it were White now to move then he might as well resign at once, since he has in fact no reasonable move. If for example *54.* K – Kt2, then there would follow *54.* .... Q – R6 ch; *55.* K – Kt1, Q – Kt5 ch, while if *54.* P – B3, then K – Kt6, in both cases with a win for Black. But in reality it is Black to move, and then it appears that he has no satisfactory tempo-move at his disposal. We are thus faced with a highly interesting position with *Zugzwang* on both sides – a rarity in actual play.

What can Black undertake when it is his turn to move and the Kings are placed on KKt1 and KR5? At first glance 53. .... Q – QB6 looks very good, but then there follows 54. K – B1 ! and so as not to allow White's King to get to K2 Black must once again play 54. .... Q – Q6 ch. Other moves are likewise inadequate, since White always replies 54. K – B1, and thus forces the Queen to return to Q6. It can be seen that in truth the problem is not so easy to solve, since Black has no satisfactory tempo-move. He must embark on a retreat with 54. .... K – Kt4 and try to lose a tempo somehow or other in the position, but this does not hold out hopes of a one hundred per cent success.

We see therefore that the right winning method does not lie in fixing the King and Queen down, without further thought. Therefore I became convinced that the position in the diagram must be examined thoroughly and systematically. So as not to complicate matters unnecessarily I started off with the assumption that neither side had a tempo-move with his pawns on the Queen's wing. This is in fact easy enough to comprehend. For if Black plays P – R4 White is forced to reply with P – R4. Otherwise P – R5 would follow and then Black would be in a position either to remain with the move by P × P or else to leave his opponent with the necessity to move by P – R6. After P – R5 White cannot capture on R4 as this would leave the pawn on B4 without defence and force a decision akin to that we shall see later in the game itself.

So, once we have made the pawn moves on the Queen's wing, there arises a position in which both sides, practically speaking, can only manoeuvre with the King. In such cases it is appropriate to follow the theory of 'corresponding squares', that is to say, for every position the White King takes up one should try to get a corresponding Black King position in which White, with the move, is in *Zugzwang* and must lose. This method is well known in pawn endings and it can be very well used here, since the ending reached is in some measure like a pawn ending. So let us embark on the next theoretical task which is indeed rich in content.

To facilitate the reader's view of the matter I will outline different variations, beginning with the simplest and clearest example. At the beginning of each analysis I show only the positions of the Kings, while the other pieces retain their places.

Position 1. White King on KKt1, Black King on KR5
This is the final position at which Black must aim. White must resign as is easy to see. After a King move *1. .... Q – R6* ch followed by *2. .... Q – Kt5* ch is decisive; the Queen has no threat of check and 1. P – B4, K – Kt6 is also hopeless.

Position 2. White King on KKt2, Black King on KKt4
Here again the win is easy to demonstrate. After *1. K – Kt1, K – R5* we have position 1, while after *1. K – R2, Q – Q5!* there is no defence against the threat of *2. .... Q × P* ch or *2. .... Q – R5* ch. That, in addition, *1. K – R1, Q – K5* ch or *1. P – B3, K – B5* is utterly hopeless needs no further proof.

Position 3. White King on KKt1, Black King on KB5
Here, too, the win is easy to perceive, since *1. K – Kt2, K – Kt4* leads to position 2, and after *1. K – R2, Q – Q2!* is immediately decisive. These three positions are easily dealt with, since White's Queen cannot obtain any opportunity of getting into play.

Position 4. White King on KKt1, Black King on KR3
Here there are two main variations, of which the second contains certain complications. We shall examine them separately.
(a) *1. K – Kt2, K – Kt4*, transposing to position 2.
(b) *1. K – R2, Q – QB6! 2. Q – K2* (*2. Q – Kt4, Q – K4* ch loses at once for White, and after *2. K – Kt2, Q – B8; 3. Q – B3, P – Q8 = Q* Black's King escapes from the checks to KR5) *2. .... Q – Q5! 3. Q – K6* ch, *K – Kt4; 4. Q – Kt8* ch (or *4. Q – K7* ch, *K – Kt5* etc.), *4. .... K – B5; 5. Q – Kt3* ch, *K – K5*, and Black's King penetrates decisively either via Q6 or KB6.

Finally, we should also mention the possibility of *1. P – B4*, which can occur as well in the second position. After this move

Black can win in various ways, of which perhaps the simplest is
1. .... Q – Kt6 ch; *2.* K – B1, Q – K6; *3.* Q – K2 (or *3.*
P – B5, K – Kt4; *4.* P – B6, K × P; *5.* Q – K2, Q – B5 ch; *6.*
K – Kt2, Q – Q5, etc. After *3.* Q – Kt4, Q – K8 ch; *4.* K – Kt2,
P – Q8 = Q White has no draw by perpetual check), *3.* ....
Q × P ch; *4.* K – Kt2, Q – Q3, and White's counter-play is
at an end.

Position 5. White King on KKt1, Black King on KB3
   Here there are three not particularly difficult variations.
   (a) *1.* K – Kt2, K – Kt4 transposing to position 2.
   (b) *1.* K – R1, Q – K5 ch; *2.* K – R2, Q – K8; *3.* Q – B3 ch,
K – K2, and Black wins.
   (c) *1.* K – R2, K – B4! *2.* Q – R5 ch (*2.* K – Kt2, K – Kt4,
or *2.* K – Kt1, K – B5, lead to either positions 2 or 3), *2.* ....
K – B5; *3.* Q – R4 ch (or *3.* Q – B7 ch, Q – B4 etc.),
3. .... K – B6, and once again Black's King penetrates in
decisive fashion.

Position 6. White King on KR2, Black King on KKt3
   With this King formation White possesses better defensive
possibilities, which are however insufficient.
   (a) *1.* K – Kt2, K – Kt4, with position 2.
   (b) *1.* K – Kt1, K – R3, with position 4.
   (c) *1.* K – R1, Q – K5 ch; *2.* K – R2, Q – K8! *3.* Q – Kt4
ch, K – B3; *4.* Q – B4 ch, K – K3; *5.* Q – Kt4 ch, K – K4,
and however White checks Black's King it reaches the Queen's
wing via Q5 or K5.
   (d) *1.* Q – Kt4 ch, K – B3; *2.* Q – B4 ch (or *2.* Q – Q1,
K – B4! with a position from variation (5c), *2.* .... K – K3; *3.*
Q – Kt4 ch (after *3.* Q – R6 ch, Black wins by *3.* ... K – Q2;
4. Q – Kt7 ch, K – Q1; *5.* Q – Kt8 ch, K – B2; *6.* Q – B7 ch,
Q – Q2 etc.), *3.* .... Q – B4! *4.* Q – Kt8 ch, K – Q2; *5.* Q –
Kt7 ch, K – B1; *6.* Q – Kt8 ch, K – Kt2; *7.* Q – Kt7 ch, K –
Kt3; *8.* Q – Kt3, Q – KB1! and Black wins.

Position 7. White King on KKt2, Black King on KKt3
   This position too is won for Black, although White possesses

THE ART OF THE MIDDLE GAME

a wealth of checks in variation d. Since the King formation in this last is important for the further course of the game, we will examine it exhaustively.

(a) *1.* K – Kt1, K – R3, with position 4.

(b) *1.* K – R1, Q – K5 ch, with a position from variation 5c.

(c) *1.* K – R2, K – B4, transposing to variation 5c.

(d) *1.* Q – Kt4 ch, K – B3; *2.* Q – B4 ch (*2.* Q – R4 ch, K – B2; *3.* Q – B4 ch, K – K1 leads to the main variation and *2.* Q – Q1, K – Kt4 to position 2), *2.* .... K – K2; *3.* Q – QB7 ch (*3.* Q – Kt5 ch, K – B2; *4.* Q – B4 ch, K – K1 results in the same variation), *3.* .... K – K3! *4.* Q × P ch (or *4.* Q – B8 ch, Q – Q2; *5.* Q – Kt8 ch, K – B3; *6.* Q – B8 ch, K – Kt3; *7.* Q – Kt8 ch, Q – Kt2; *8.* Q – Q8, K – B4 dis ch, and Black wins), *4.* .... Q – Q3; *5.* Q – K4 ch (the other possibility, *5.* Q – K8 ch, K – B3; *6.* Q – R8 ch, K – Kt3; *7.* Q – Kt8 ch, K – B4; *8.* Q – B7 ch, K – Kt4, would lose just as well after *9.* P – B4 ch, K – R3; as after *9.* Q – Kt7 ch, Q – Kt3 etc.), *5.* .... K – B3; *6.* Q – B3 ch (or *6.* Q – R4 ch, K – Kt2 etc.), *6.* .... K – Kt4! *7.* Q – K3 ch (*7.* Q – Q1, Q – Q6 gives us variation 2), *7.* .... K – Kt3; *8.* Q – K8 ch, K – Kt2, and Black wins.

Position 8. White King on KKt2, Black King on KB4

After the above variations have been investigated we now come to the most important position of our analysis. This can also arise from position 2 through the move *1.* .... K – B4 and it shows thereby that position 2 is absolutely won for Black, entirely irrespective as to whose turn it is to move. If we can also demonstrate that position 8 is won for Black, then we can regard our work as ended. Let us have a look at the various possibilities.

(a) *1.* K – Kt1, K – B5, with position 3.

(b) *1.* K – R1, Q – K5 ch; *2.* K – R2, Q – R5 ch, followed by *3.* .... Q – Kt5 ch, etc.

(c) *1.* K – R2, Q – Q5; *2.* Q – R5 ch, K – K5; *3.* Q – Kt6 ch (*3.* Q – K2 ch, K – B5), *3.* .... K – B6, and Black's King penetrates with decisive effect.

(d) *1.* Q – R5 ch, K – B3; *2.* Q – R4 ch (*2.* Q – Q1, K – Kt4

leads to position 2 and after *2.* Q – R8 ch, K – B2 the checks
are at an end), *2. .... * K – B2; *3.* Q – B4 ch, K – K1; *4.*
Q – Kt8 ch, K – Q2; *5.* Q – Kt7 ch, K – K3! transposing to the
method of winning in variation 7d.

Thus we have demonstrated the win in this important position,
and have eventually acquired the knowledge as to what way we
must proceed in the game in order to win by a logical method.
The right way should be *49. .... * K – B3; *50.* K – Kt1, P – R4;
51. P – R4, K – Kt4; *52.* K – Kt2, K – B4! and Black wins
as the analysis of position 8 demonstrated beyond all doubt.
This plan can always be realized, since White is forced to play
his King to KKt2 once the Black monarch has advanced to
KKt4, and thereupon follows K – B4, etc. It therefore also
follows that White is unable in any event to defend his position,
however skilfully he may still manoeuvre with his King.

49. ....   K – Kt3

Now perhaps the reader might ask why in fact Black does not
follow the set plan and play the logical *49. .... * K – B3; *50.*
K – Kt1, P – R4, etc., as we have shown above, but instead
embarks on another continuation? The reasons are purely
practical. We have seen that Black, in the main variation 8d can
put up a stern resistance with the aid of numerous checks. Hence
Black first tries other ways so as to see if White has gained a
comprehension of the right defensive ideas. These tactics are
quite without risk as Black always has the possibility of transposing play into variation 8. The idea of the text-move lies in
first trying to obtain one of the winning King positions in variations 1–8, before the pawn position on the Queen's wing has
become blocked. As we have come to see, this has a certain
importance and may make the winning method noticeably
easier if the opponent does not defend himself in the best way.
With the text-move Black is forced to transpose to the winning
variation 4 after *50.* K – Kt1, K – R3, and he also allows White
to play *50.* Q – Kt4 ch, which at the same time means transposing to the winning variation 8.

50. K – Kt1   K – R3
51. K – Kt2?

231

Here, however, *51.* P – R3 was necessary so as to answer *51.* .... P – R4 with *52.* P – R4. In that event Black would have had nothing better than to transpose to variation 8 by *52.* .... K – Kt4; *53.* K – Kt2, K – B4. The reason why White should play P – R3 before Black gets in P – R4 becomes clear in the game.

> *51.* ....   K – Kt4

Black does not notice his opportunity. With *51.* .... P – R4 he could have finished off the game without further complications. If White then were to play *52.* P – R4 we would come after *52.* .... K – Kt4 to the winning variation 2, and after *52.* P – R3, P – R5! *53.* P × P, Q – B6 is decisive, since now *54.* K – B1 will not do on account of *54.* .... Q × P ch. Finally, if White continues with *52.* K – Kt1, then Black plays *52.* .... P – R5 and wins easily, since by P × P or P – R6 he can, just as he likes, allow a *Zugzwang* position to either White or Black.

After the move played White could again have played *52.* P – R3. Since he has once again neglected this opportunity Black wins the ending without further complications.

> *52.* K – Kt1   P – R4!

Keres

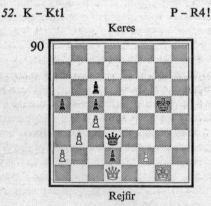

90

Rejfir

Now it becomes clear why Black refrained from the immediate blocking of the pawns on his Queen's wing. The move played guarantees him the requisite tempo however White now plays, and forces the win without any trouble. Perhaps White had reckoned only with *52. .... K – R5* and in reply to this intended to defend himself by *53. P – R3*.

> **53. K – Kt2**

There is no longer any defence. After *53. P – R4, K – R5 Zugzwang*, and *53. P – R3* allows the finish *53. .... P – R5; 54. P × P, Q – Q5; 55. K – B1, Q × QBP ch;* followed by *56. .... Q – Kt5 ch* and exchange of Queens.

> **53. ....**   **P – R5**
> **54. P × P**

Desperation, but there was nothing to be done. After *54. K – Kt1*, Black wins by *54. .... P × P; 55. P × P, K – R5*, and after *54. K – R2*, there comes *54. .... K – R5; 55. K – Kt1, P – R6*. One sees how useful it is for Black's plans to have a pawn on QR5.

> **54. ....**   **Q – K5 ch**
> **55. K – B1**

Or *55. P – B3, Q – K8, etc.*

> **55. ....**   **Q × P ch**
> **56. K – Kt2**   **Q – Kt5 ch**
>   **resigns.**

A very instructive ending from the analytical point of view. It shows in the first place how one can and must work out a winning method in a position where the opponent has only a few defensive possibilities. In the second it should be definitely noted that it is not always appropriate to employ at once the prepared winning method, if one can first lay some stumbling blocks in the opponent's way by another line. A pre-condition is that the position is not hazarded in any way, and that one is able to transpose back into the prepared winning variation later on.

The examples I have given above are not designed to yield anything like an entirely systematic book of rules as to how one should analyse an adjourned game. My purpose was merely to show the sort of work that awaits a chess-master at home after he has adjourned a game. Perhaps also this chapter may serve to give other masters occasion to communicate their experiences in this respect, and so we will have illuminated a territory in the game of chess to which earlier chess literature has hardly devoted any attention.

INDEX OF PLAYERS

236

INDEX OF PLAYERS

INDEX OF MIDDLE-GAME THEMES

THE GAME OF CHESS

H. Golombek

'This is the best value of any chess book that I know and gives a clear and comprehensive exposition of the game' – C. H. O'D. Alexander in the *Sunday Times*

'A lucid and logical introduction to the game . . . sound instruction all the way through' – *The Times Literary Supplement*

Mr Golombek's concise survey of the fundamentals of chess has quickly established itself as a classic of chess literature. Since 1954 it has sold over 190,000 copies. This new edition has been thoroughly revised and brought up to date. The section on openings now includes the most modern of all openings, the Robatsch defence, and an entirely new chapter has been added on the younger school, with particular reference to Fischer and Tal.